AS_____

PROJECTION

GUIDE

BOOK ONE

By

Yvette A. LeBlanc

This book, Astral Projection Guide, Book One, is dedicated to my family who mean everything to me.

And I must confess that if any credit is due from this it really belongs to my spiritual guides who constantly inspired me, guided me on my astral projection adventures, and then practically wrote it.

TABLE OF CONTENTS

Foreword

As a young child, many vivid dreams of jumping down my front-hall staircase without touching the stairs and floating over a grassy hill gave me a firm conviction that I was like Peter Pan and could fly. And guess what, we can all fly and I can tell you how using astral projection.

During my mid-twenties, while giving myself self-hypnotic commands to relax, I very unexpectedly, while fully awake, floated above my body for a few moments. I was a sphere of energy and light and could see in all directions at once. This earth-shaking experience started my quest for knowledge and thirst for more such experiences. Due to the kindness of my spiritual guides, I have now had many exciting astral projection and inner world adventures. I feel compelled to share this wisdom and my stories, both awesome and difficult, with you.

I now realize that physical life is a lot like a movie that we compose, produce, star in, and direct, but it is a temporary production. Our essence, beautiful light and energy, is permanent and the part of us that is capable of traveling to many other realities. Our true being (who we really are) is usually located on the skin right between the eyes not even inside our heads. Our physical bodies are simply vehicles needed to experience the physical plane.

Astral projection can help eliminate a fear of death because, if you choose and ask for the wisdom, you will know for certain we are all eternal, each a single cell in the magnificent body of God.

It is my belief that each one of us, through our own free will, has created and then chosen this distorted physical existence to learn the lessons that only a belief in a beginning and an ending can bring. I can think of no other reason. If you choose to find the truth, you will learn we all have a vibrant, healthy existence apart from our physical reality which is only a very small part of us.

I know that time is an illusion because I have time-traveled backwards and been an active participant. I believe I have also traveled to the future, but it very easily could have been to another reality. Who can tell for sure?

Everyone willing to invest some time can easily and safely have many exciting astral projections. The amount of time needed varies from person to person depending on any natural ability. Sniffing glue, taking drugs, or eating hallucinogenic mushrooms is not only unnecessary but will cause distortions in your trip, and who knows what the health costs might be. By following the simple and direct methods I teach, you can journey to the astral counterparts of the past, present, and future and to other dimensions. My techniques involve deep breathing, asserting the positive, spiritual meditation, and visualization.

It is not an emptying of all your life force from your physical body and leaving behind a shell; if it were, you would not survive the trip. It is instead a separation. There is the part of you who needs to breathe quietly and stays behind and the part of you who leaves and has an amazing adventure. You remain as safe as when asleep.

It is through deep, holy meditation and prayer that we can become blessed with the assistance of great spiritual beings. We need their help. When it comes to astral projection, you and I are in kindergarten; our guides, however, have their doctorates. We become volunteer work for these awesome higher beings. I can show you some easy and basic ways to get out of your body, but it is your guides who will take you on your astral adventures.

On a scale of one to ten, one being the projection that happens when you glance at something, ten being an astral projection that is just as real to you as things are right now while reading this book, of course, your goal is ten. It might be very easy for you or, like me, you might have to become determined and put some effort into it, but everyone can do this. When you reach 7, 8, or 9 on that scale, you will have longer and more vivid flashes of other realities.

There are probably as many techniques as there are people who project; and you will also develop your own methods. However, you can learn a lot from what I and others have found on our pathways.

Sometime back in the 1960's, before I understood what LSD was, I took a metaphysical correspondence course. I found it very enlightening and after a while I dropped my guard. One day in the mail I received a little white pill from these people. I was very young and gullible. I actually thought it must be some special herb that was gathered at the time of the full moon. I swallowed it and laid myself down. Very shortly, without any effort, I had an astral projection to Medjugorje and viewed Mother Mary talking to some young people. She did not look in my direction. I was awe stricken to be in her presence, but I knew I was not welcome and did not belong there. I felt like an intruder. Believe me; it is so much more rewarding to have an astral projection without the use of drugs.

If you honestly believe you cannot do astral projection, this book is written for you. It gives extremely detailed instruction using some basic techniques designed for EVERYONE to succeed. I have also explained some pathways to build up confidence.

Aura viewing is also covered. It involves gazing into a mirror and seeing your astral and etheric light and your golden halo. You might also find sacred symbols embedded in your aura. You'll be amazed at how easy it is and at what you will see even on the first attempt. If you can see your energy extending from your physical body, then you know you can float on top of it because a part of you does that all the time. An easy confidence-building technique is given where you will start by floating only your two feet upward. Looking at your own magnificent light and then floating above your physical expression are life altering experiences and prove you are indeed a child of God.

By following this guidance, I believe you will more fully understand why we're here and how to benefit from the Earth experience. My beliefs and yours and everyone else's can be so different and yet we all start and will eventually end at the very same place, the Godhead (which we really never leave, we just think we do). It's good to understand these things so our attention is on the spiritual and not on the material. Just writing these words helps my focus.

You think you can't do astral projection? I had those feelings once, so I can certainly relate. Follow my instructions, put in the necessary time, and you will find yourself projecting to wherever and whenever your focus dictates on the astral, etheric, and spiritual planes. Sometimes you'll be real close to the physical, sometimes not.

All the techniques I teach are easy and basic. You can do these things if you really choose, but you need to put it on your "front burner" as far as your attention and time scheduling go. It's a matter of building up and maintaining a momentum of spiritual energy. If you have problems, schedule your practice times closer together. If I haven't done astral projection in a while, to gain the necessary momentum of energy, I schedule two or three sessions a day until projection just happens with my focus.

You can travel anywhere to any dimension or time you choose, because a part of you is already in every place and every time is really the present moment. If you persist you will discover this truth for yourself.

For me, and probably you, the length of each session depends on whether I fall asleep or whether an overwhelming burst of energy comes and wakes me back up to the physical. You'll find your own pathway. And then, like me, you'll probably feel compelled to share. I hope you do. I want to read your book.

This guidance for both astral projection and aura viewing and the accounts of many of my adventures were first written by me some years ago for a series of magazine articles that never materialized. I then sadly had other matters that took up most of my energy. When I decided to publish this material, to verify everything I said earlier, I started over as a beginner. I had to rediscover my own teachings, inspired by my spiritual guides, which lead to the most profound, intense and life changing experiences. It pains me to know that over time I abandoned this wisdom to concentrate on what is more mundane. This book is therefore written from both the teacher's and the student's perspective.

If you start to have visions and possibly hear voices, and you probably will if you regularly practice what's in this book, and if you change your mind and want them to stop, simply stop practicing the techniques, assert out loud that you wish them to stop, and they will then start to go away. However, just like it usually takes time to develop this ability, it could take some time for these interruptions to stop. So you are about to make a very serious, life-altering decision.

Part One of this book gives basic information in preparation for astral projection to the inner and outer astral worlds. Part Two gives many different concise and detailed instructions, leaving you with freedom to choose the pathway that is best suited for you. Part Three tells of my adventures, both spiritual and traumatic, so you will have an idea of what to expect. Part Four digs into the aura, etheric, and halo lights and contains a basic viewing technique which will give you tremendous confidence that you can leave the physical because a part of you already has. You will find my instructions are very concise with basic information and a multitude of techniques. I explain what you need to know, what to expect, and how to do it. This book is simple and direct.

I frequently ask for general guidance for the promotion of my writings. I am usually told that, since on the material side of life I already have the basics, the practical part should be of little use to me. This physical life that seems so important now will just fade into a dream later. What's important is that I write these teachings down so that I can remember and relate to them better. There are many other sources for this guidance for you my readers. Everyone is on his/her own pathway and will have the knowledge and guidance necessary always at just the perfect time. When I persist, they tell me that the outcome will be whatever I truly expect and desire it to be. I have to learn to either let go or ask very specific questions.

I have found over and over that the answers to my prayers come not only in lucid dreams and inspiration but also in the form of events of the physical world. Sometimes these experiences can be very difficult to endure, but if analyzed carefully can turn into answers. It's why we're here, to learn.

In January of 2013 I wrote a paper designed to help those who were still having difficulties with astral projection. Then I incorporated these even easier techniques into this book. In March and May of 2014 I wrote further updates. In August of 2014 I sadly took down a book on lucid dreaming with more instruction for astral projection because it wasn't selling. I have included that information into this updated version. In 2015 I updated this material on a regular basis.

I hope you enjoy reading it. I certainly enjoyed writing it.

PART ONE, BASIC INFORMATION

Definitions

Ancient through present-day, metaphysical wisdom has come to us from many sources resulting in a slight semantic problem. Different experts and traditions occasionally have varied meanings for the same words. Because it can sometimes be confusing and distracting, I offer some brief definitions of words and phrases as used in this book.

The following is my understanding; others might have different definitions and relate to things in their own ways. And you, too, will have your own approach to these mysteries, if you don't already. It's difficult to label and explain because the boundaries of the astral and etheric worlds are not as clear as the physical plane.

The acronym "obe" stands for out-of-body experience. It basically means that part of you, your true being, will leave your physical body and travel in a sphere of energy to another reality, sometimes very close to the physical, sometimes far from it. I will use the verb "project" to define the act of having an obe (also referred to as astral projection)>

Everything that's alive has an etheric counterpart. You can sometimes see it as a white light extending about a couple of inches from one side when practicing aura viewing techniques. It has the same size and shape as the physical and is very closely connected to this plane. Sometimes if you stare at your head in the mirror, it can be seen as a whitish glow. It is your ghost. Of all your nonphysical bodies, it can be viewed the most easily. However, it can get a bit confusing because it sometimes reflects the light of your aura, clothing, hair, and especially your golden halo.

The lower etheric plane is a place where danger is usually found everywhere. If you have an astral projection while centered in your lower etheric body, you can and should raise your vibrations and change your trip for the better by looking upward and searching for vibrant rainbow colors and brilliant white light. It won't be difficult. There is also a high etheric, a spiritual plane with awesome white light sparkling with flashes of rainbow colors. I consider it to be the very highest of heavens. This is where you can find unbelievably beautiful spiritual beings. A few times I have been so overwhelmed and so grateful to be in their presence I just trembled. If you look, you can also find your own Christ Self there. Some authorities label this plane instead as a high astral or spiritual plane. And, I believe, there are many etheric planes in between.

The astral plane is a vibration of life that is highly emotional and visiting it can be a nightmare world of hell, a blissful journey to heaven, or one of many, many places in between.. Because we have an astral projection using an astral body, we should expect to have emotional experiences. We possess different energies of all vibrations; and will, without realizing or making any effort, choose just the correct combination depending on the vibration of light needed for the journey.

Astral energy and life can sometimes be seen on the physical plane as flashes of different colored light and it sometimes blends with the etheric. It could reflect astral life beyond our comprehension, our own aura, our own positive or negative thought forms, positive or negative thoughts directed to us from others, the presence of the deceased, angels, guides, and on and on.

The borderland is a hallucinogenic plane between our reality and the astral and etheric worlds. It is where people intoxicated on alcohol or drugs visit. You can also create this distorted place if your intentions are not righteous.

The word "chakra" comes to us from the Hindu and Buddhist teachings. Simply defined, they are swirling centers of energy and light located, I believe, in the astral. Some place them in the etheric. It is widely accepted that there are seven major chakras and many minor ones. My belief is that the first four major chakras are located along the spinal cord: at the very bottom, at the points corresponding to the middle of the stomach, the bottom of the rib cage, and the very center of the chest. The three higher are at the center of the throat, the middle of the head, and just above the very top of the head. There are other teachings that say the heart chakra is located where the physical heart is located.

Except for the throat chakra which, most experts agree, is colored blue, the colors vary from teacher to teacher. And there are many different beliefs pertaining to minor chakras as to their location, color and meaning.

Practical Use

I don't consider the astral projection experience to be physical-world accurate enough for scientific research nor for financial or stock market guidance. You would be trying to force the astral body to be in a realm where it is not designed to operate; doing so could create a borderland of illusion.

It's very difficult for the astral body to deal with a mundane task. From my experience, when you enter the astral plane, you'll be much more emotional than you usually are and will want to do things like flying and visiting other more interesting realms. Putting on your astral body is in some emotional ways like becoming a young child again.

Obviously, it's the best way to visit those who have passed on. You can even settle things by extending love and forgiveness. Just keep in mind that the deceased, having a vibrant, very important life beyond our understanding, are not just hanging around up there waiting for our visits. And sometimes there is only a short period of time before they reincarnate. Of course, be careful not to encourage haunting. Contacting my parents using astral projection has given me great comfort.

Personally, I don't think an astral projection should be used to locate a missing person or valued object. You might be very successful but then again your attempts could also do more damage than good, especially if you are emotionally involved. The physical body is designed to deal with the physical plane. When you use an astral vehicle, you might find what you expect to find and not what is there from the physical perspective. If I wanted to locate someone or something in physical reality, I would rely instead on dowsing techniques that incorporate the use of a map. There are lots of good books on that subject.

And, of course, astral projection is the only way to time and dimension travel, to fly, and to visit an astral counterpart of a spirit or physical object or place.

Dweller on the Threshold

The following is my belief based on my own personal experiences and research. .

In early lifetimes, most have committed evil deeds that would shock and hinder progress if known about now in our more refined states. Unless you're a saint, this dark side is still with you and needs to be addressed. Made of the densest etheric matter and separated for the sake of our sanity, it still maintains some of our life force, has movement, and a separate but very closely linked intelligence. It has control over our negative thought forms and will tempt us at every opportunity.

We have probably made much progress, but some lessons are still waiting, otherwise we would not be here on the Earth plane. With a fierce determination, this being holds us to the Earth and lower astral planes.

You can feel the pull of negativity on the physical, called gravity. An extremely holy person can walk on water and levitate because these energies have been conquered. Of course, there are teachings in the bible of Beloved Jesus walking on water. Tradition teaches that Saint Teresa of Avila (1515 – 1582) sometimes in deep meditation did not touch the ground but floated above. And I understand there are accounts of Hindu saints who have levitated and might still be levitating.

The presence of the Dweller on the physical is also reflected in us through disease and death. I know with me sometimes I have intense cravings for food that I know is not healthy and will do me damage.

On the astral or emotional plane, this pull is called by such names as depression, anxiety, anger, guilt, fear, etc.

The Dweller wants us to fail because then the separation diminishes and it gains dominion; the holier we become the less power it has and considers that its death. It wants us to exist only in the lower astral plane where it can gain total control, the state of existence called hell, where it becomes our tormenting devil.

When you are very relaxed and ready to have an astral projection, do not be surprised to receive a visit from the Dweller. Even though it sometimes presents itself as a very ugly monster, if we understand it, it should not be feared; it's part of us. It could use a multitude of ploys: for instance, just before an astral projection, it's a common occurrence to hear clear voices saying things like: "There's a fire in the house." "Your children are in danger." After you have responded several times by getting up and checking, you will find, if you pay no further attention, the ploy will stop.

We all have temptations to overcome that act as anchors to the Earth plane. Meditation and astral projection force us to deal with them. Organized by the Dweller, these weaknesses exist on the lower astral plane and try to prevent us from progress. They are called negative thought forms and have a life, color and form; they are alive and very confused. Mentally send them light and they will be transformed into energies that will lead to higher planes instead. They usually appear as snakes like mine have.

Once in a great while, for our own good, our guides allow us to see these negative thought forms from the astral plane which does not mean we're on a bad trip. It's good to view our own negativity in this manner, even though it is shocking. It helps to give us the whole picture. I have found such visions help combat negative temptations. I suggest you simply accept any such experience for the lesson it is meant to be. However, if you are on such a trip, and want it to stop, say "no" out loud and move your physical fingers and toes. Any such trip will then stop immediately.

During one of my visions I saw my negativity appear to me as a three-headed snake. One of the heads mouthed the very words that were traveling through my head at the time. (I was trying to talk myself out of doing my daily meditation.) Believe me that vision has helped me a lot to understand and overcome. On an astral projection adventure or lucid dream, if you feel you are part of the negative energy, end your trip immediately. If you are watching it from a distance with your guides, that's a whole different story and my advice is to trust your guides.

Basics

Your physical body is the vehicle designed to help you live on the physical plane. It's similar to an automobile or an airplane with you as the driver. When you leave the physical you might stay close but you'll be in an astral, spiritual, or etheric body, usually an astral, so during an astral projection to a physical object or place expect to see some distortion because you won't be using the vehicle designed for the physical plane.

If you read books on the subject, you'll find different people might contradict and explain things from their own individual perspectives. The whole subject of astral projection and lucid dreaming is nowhere near scientific; sometimes it just works like we expect.

I can think of no other reason for being on Planet Earth than to grow in wisdom by experiencing beginnings and endings over and over. Our focus takes us here and there to learn and so we make progress. It's like a game of monopoly. When you visit any of the heaven worlds like I have, you'll learn life here really doesn't matter as much as we presume it does. The wisdom gained from etheric and astral projections and lucid dreams helps to make the many challenges here on Earth much easier to manage.

We live on the planet of free will. Life is what we make of it. If you put astral projection and lucid dreaming on your "front burner" and take it step by step you'll learn so much of what reality really is. It's beyond explanation. The experience of astral projection starting from either the waking or the sleeping state will change you forever. If you want to go ever and ever deeper, remember your goal at the onset and focus, focus, focus.

To help make astral projection and lucid dreaming more doable, during your daily routine pause, visualize and breathe in positive colors. Recognize that you are a piece of the vastness of the Light of God. Decorate your meditation and sleeping areas with pictures or items that reflect these colors so you can study them just before your attempt. This meditation on rainbow colors and white while deep breathing can become your bridge to both astral projection and lucid dreaming.

A further step towards your goal would be to meditate on your union with all of God's creation, thus adding to the huge pool of love here on Mother Earth and also drawing on it. We all share the same atoms in the air we breathe which are swept throughout this creation on the Earth plane by the wind. We also share the light from our auras and our thoughts. When one person flourishes spiritually, we all grow. Because of all this sharing, when we have an astral projection to a different time or place, we find part of us is already there.

A spirit who appeared to be from ancient Egypt visited me one time. He advised to breathe in the golden light if I want good health. I found his advice worked; it proved to be very healing. The next step that seemed only logical to me was to breathe in the other rainbow-colored and white lights. I now use this technique during my preparation time because it makes the process a lot easier.

Do not be concerned if you are afraid of heights; you won't be when you project. An astral projection adventure of flying off a tall mountain or into deep space will be exhilarating and not scary.

And most important, don't get discouraged. Unless you're blessed with a gift, for the rest of us dealing with the astral is like a child going through school; you make the effort and take it one step at a time. When you focus on it, your pathway will open to you making it not only manageable but easy and very exciting.

We are able to leave the physical body in that very relaxed moment between sleeping and waking. Approached from the waking state, it is a fairly deep meditation; from the sleeping, a lucid dream. Both, of course, initially appeal to different people. Once you make progress using one approach, the other becomes easier as well.

To have an astral projection from the waking state, my advice is don't get hung up with tedious, drawn-out methods to leave your physical body one body part at a time. You don't need to project an astral counterpart of your entire physical self as in some teachings. The exception, of course, is when you float on top of your physical body, an amazing experience that I will teach later in this book.

Most often, I suggest you simply project that part of you located between your eyes. If you pause and think about it, from this very basic perspective, we're really a small ball of energy located there most of the time anyway. The physical body is a vehicle for this ball of life to understand and relate to the physical world.

A fast and easy way out is to just focus intently on wherever it is you want to be. Don't even consider what you look like. Once you're at your destination and satisfied with the intensity, you can change your size if you choose. It sure is amazing to see the world from the perspective of a small sphere of light.

One mistaken belief that might prevent you from having an astral projection is that you cannot separate from the part of you that breathes. The way to get over that fear is to use your breath instead as a tool to leave. You'll notice in my techniques they all are based first on deep breathing. You breathe deeply until you are so filled with oxygen that your breath naturally slows way down and you can pause very briefly on the exhale, your way out. There will be the part of you that continues to breathe softly and the part of you that has your astral adventure. Your physical body will tell you when it needs your attention to supply more oxygen, sometimes ending your trip, sometimes you will just continue to be divided into two, the part that breathes and the part who does not. If the need for breathing ends your trip, it's usually easy to return after an additional period of deep breathing. This is why drugs that slow down the breath artificially work for astral projection, but obviously not a healthy pathway.

If you are sleep deprived, attempts to meditate will just bring you to sleep which is okay. You can project from the sleeping state into a lucid dream which then usually becomes an inner obe.

If you choose to start your astral projection from the dream state, frequently during your daily routine (out loud if possible) pause and say something like "I am awake and now in control." If statements like this are a habit during your waking life, they will flow more easily into your dream state as well. As you go to sleep at night, assert out loud that you will remember your dreams and be able to manipulate them. Once you start to doze, I suggest you try to fly.

And then these two approaches just blend together anyway. You can easily fall asleep into a vivid dream that starts from the waking state; and you can wake from the sleeping state to continue your astral projection adventure.

There is one other thing I want to emphasize before you get started. Even the most amazing astral projections happen in a matter-of-fact manner. There probably will be no bells ringing, no choirs of angels singing. Sometimes it will take a little while to digest the experience and realize what happened.

The practice of spiritual meditation is paramount to build up the necessary momentum of energy. Schedule this time so that immediately beforehand you will be doing calming activities. It took me a while to realize that watching a detective mystery on television right before my meditation was not helpful. I could project but it was in high speed. Everything moved very fast, not what I wanted. It took a major effort on my part to slow things down.

One practice that works very well for me is the memory of the feeling of touching things. However, on the astral and etheric planes that you will be visiting unless you choose otherwise there is no touch only the memory of it because on those levels we can pass through whatever appears without feeling anything. You will experience what you want and expect. By bringing the memory of touch along with me it helps my astral projections and dreams to become more intense.

I have found that the more mundane (like stock market guidance) or boring the trip, the harder it will be because our guides won't really be very interested. Personal privacy is respected by our guides, so they won't help you travel to a neighbor's house. I have tried to project to the same vase countless times. You'd think it would get easier, but it seems to get harder. I think it's because my guides get bored. There are very detailed instructions to have an astral projection to an object in a room later in this book. Try it. It'll change you forever. When I do it, I'm tiny and the vase is gigantic.

Your guides will want to bring you to places like past lifetimes, to one of the heavens, to alternate lives, someplace where you will benefit spiritually. They might want you to be of help to those in dire emotional need. I have traveled to past, future, and alternate lifetimes (usually I can't tell the difference), slipped inside willing people and helped them in times of severe emotional distress. I have learned very valuable lessons from these travels. (Because of this I believe time and space are illusions.) I suggest you select a general type of trip or dream and let your guides choose the specifics. They really know what's best.

If our attention is mostly on the light and love of God throughout our day and also into the evening time, our physical life gets easier and happier while astral projection and lucid dreaming both become more attainable.

Pray for signs that your path to astral projection is correct for you and follow your own inner guidance. If you want to astral project and have lucid dreams, like any other positive accomplishment, pray, focus, and become very determined.

I'm neither special nor gifted, if I can do this, you can, too.

Different Bodies

The concept of having different energies (bodies or vehicles) available is a fairly new one for the western world, but the Hindus have taught just that for thousands of years. In Manly P. Hall's book, Unseen Forces (Philosophical Research Society, Inc., Copyright

1978), he explains we have four types of vehicles: the physical, etheric, astral and mental.

When you have your astral projection, you will usually be in an astral body so expect highly emotional trips. An etheric projection, from my experience, will bring you to a place that is all foggy white and much harder to understand than the astral plane. It's easier to do a full-bodied projection from the etheric, which would be your ghost.

The Theosophical Society also reports that to leave lower emotions behind we can project upward from our astral body to the mental body (sometimes called the high etheric). Two other advantages are that you will be more focused and will have a much more spiritually oriented adventure.

I suggest you don't focus or even question what type of body you are in during an astral projection, just enjoy the trip.

Intent

Intention is everything. Be positive and both your astral and physical worlds will improve. If you try to force yourself to do something even borderline evil, boring or repetitious during an astral projection, your chances of success are pretty small. Our guides are the ones really in control and get bored with us sometimes. And they certainly shy away from some of the things that might interest us like financial matters or what a neighbor is doing.

Positive astral energy can be seen as beautiful spheres of light, heard as a popping noise, felt like vibrations of electricity and can be magnified by focusing on it. Sometimes as it passes through our physical bodies it causes an itch, twitch, or a shudder.

Negative astral energy can sometimes be seen as snakes or gargoyle-like figures, colored blood red, black, brown, or grey which can be transmuted into a violet color (forgiveness and mercy) through visualization.

Other Realities

It's possible to visit a myriad of other realities in what is considered to be the present, past, future, and parallel universes including many different heavens and hells. When you do so, you will realize that time, space, form, even the concept of an inside and an outside are all illusions we have created to experience physical life in an orderly manner. The past and future become the present moment, because there is nothing but the present moment.

When we time travel, we are in an astral vehicle so our astral projection will be emotional, sometimes to very rough times. The good old days for most of us were usually not so good.

You will find that oftentimes when you astral travel you will be an active participant in these realities, probably a volunteer. You could slip into the consciousness of another and take control for a few moments or longer usually to help an individual deal with an extremely difficult event like a death, sometimes their own or a loved one.

Sometimes during an astral projection it's a challenge to figure out if we are in the present, future, past or alternate reality because in an astral projection we just get a piece of the picture. From my experience, we seem to have a myriad of existences all going on at once. I believe what we consider to be our present is simply where our focus happens to be.

To time and dimension travel we must deal with the free will of our guides, the people visited, and sometimes that of an alternate self. To relate to another physical-appearing reality, usually we need to slip into the being of another. Think about it. When would you welcome someone from another reality entering your consciousness? It would probably be only at moments of intense grief, pain, fear, or death. With very few exceptions, when I have time traveled, it has been to such very painful places.

If you choose to have an astral projection only to happier times, make the request out loud at the very first stage when practicing any of my techniques.

Vivid Projection

Since vivid projection from the waking state usually entails first going into a deep meditative trance, if you are sleep deprived you will probably just go to sleep, but possibly to a lucid dream. Vivid, astral projection from the waking state requires one to be both fully alert and fully relaxed.

Those who consume caffeine or lots of sugar could be too wound up to relax enough to have an astral projection.

Digesting meat and fish brings on a heavy, sluggish feeling, making astral projection more difficult than it has to be. The creatures that have been eaten have usually suffered a painful death and the essence of fear stays in the flesh even after it has been cooked and may have a very negative influence on a projection. If you have vivid nightmares, this could be your problem.

I have found a mostly vegan, organic diet consisting of lots of raw greens, raw fruits, vegetables, nuts and seeds has a very positive effect. Eating in this manner means a lighter and more energetic feeling throughout your body making it easier for astral projection in a healthy manner.

People who will find it the easiest to project have a natural ability (sometimes earned from a previous or alternate lifetime), are in the habit of frequent meditation and prayer, and can control their minds. However, everybody can have vivid, life-altering astral projection adventures, some with more and some with less ease. Like me, you might have to put some time and effort into it.

You need to know you can do it, be willing to master the techniques, build up a certain momentum of energy through spiritual meditation, deep breathing, and chanting. You should also request one or more spiritual guides to help, and always follow your own inner intuition.

The more energy and focus you give it, the wider and stronger the pathway will open for you.

High Spiritual Guides

An astral projection adventure that is planned and controlled by your guides should be expected because it is your guides who will know the best times and places to take you. OBE and inner-world travel is really a group effort.

Sometimes I extend a lot of energy trying unsuccessfully to project, but then instead I get a vivid dream later that night or I'm blessed with an astral projection first thing in the morning as I wake. The conclusion I have come to is that the timing of an obe is not always ours to decide because we're on the schedule of our guides.

Request help by praying out loud for their assistance, and then always be grateful to them. I strongly suggest you don't attempt astral projection without them. They offer protection and wisdom.

Most of the time, while on a trip, I don't even notice the presence of these wondrous beings. It's later when I do a mental review of the trip that I realize somebody had to be guiding me.

Usually when we have an astral projection it will be in energy that is highly emotional, so expect very emotional experiences, both positive and horrific. To raise the energy level, look upward for beautiful light.

Under the guidance of high spiritual guides there will always be a lesson to be learned or a task to be completed. Spiritual progress will always be made. A trip planned and directed by your guides is a most valuable treasure and blessing. If you have the highest and purest intentions, they will be eager to assist, because in this way they can also grow spiritually.

If your desires are not pure and of the highest spiritual intent, then you could attract low-type spirits who are looking for a good laugh at your expense or even some evil beings, and that at best would be a waste of time. And heaven help you on any trips they might have up their sleeves.

Healthy Astral Projections

It is my understanding that the reason people have prolonged astral projections who have consumed mind-altering drugs, eaten hallucinogenic mushrooms, or sniffed glue is that these substances can induce an anesthetizing effect on the body resulting in the breath slowing down way too much. Consequently, these people do not feel the need to breathe anywhere near as much as is necessary. Due to a lack of oxygen, the blood drains from their faces and they appear to be very ill or even dead while on their extended but much distorted trips. Obviously, that is not a healthy approach. To have a healthy astral projection starting from the waking state, it is the time directly after chanting and during deep breathing spent on the out breath as well as the pause after the out breath that will become your doorway to many exciting astral projection adventures.

To get to this place where you can project, you must become very relaxed so that tension is released; spend time chanting and deep breathing; sometimes you will almost start to doze. You will be so full of oxygen that your breathing naturally slows way down and the pause on the out breath extends almost without your notice, called by some the trance state. It is then through deep meditation and a very positive attitude that it becomes possible to separate from the part of you who continues to gently breathe.

Become so relaxed from this holy deep breathing that you feel heavy and filled with electricity. After a while, your body will tell you that it needs more oxygen and you will start to awaken from your trance. At this time, do more deep breathing and chanting. The second or more round will be to an even deeper trance state. The deeper the trance and the more focused you become, the easier the astral projection either outward or inward will be.

You will hear a ringing in your ears, feel heaviness and something akin to electricity run throughout your body--all signs that you are raising your vibrations, necessary for astral projection. You'll find the ringing will follow wherever your attention takes you within your physical body. You will even hear the ringing noise softly in the background later throughout your daily activities. If you want the ringing to either end or become less noisy, you'll have to stop meditating.

A shortcut to the necessary heavy feeling is to lie on your stomach with your hands facing down, bent at the wrists, and located under your shoulders. Move only your chest and your arms up and down with your waist stationary--like abbreviated push ups. Do as many as you comfortably can; then assume your chosen position. You'll notice heaviness throughout your body. This exercise will shorten your preparation time quite a bit.

Focus on love for All That Is, our Creator, our God.

Energy for Astral Projections

Astral projection is possible by utilizing energy obtained from very focused deep, rhythmic breathing and chanting which can be heard, felt and seen. It makes a ringing noise of various pitches; sometimes you'll hear a snap or a pop; it feels somewhat like electricity racing through your body. You can see it when the screen your eyelids make when your eyes are closed seems to contain an energy that is alive and sometimes becomes full of very intensely beautiful spheres of multicolored light.

By paying attention to this energy, it can be augmented for astral projection. It is not an unusual experience for the intensity to get so great that you feel paralyzed. If that happens and you want it to stop, just mentally say "no" and move your fingers and/or your toes. Although it's certainly not necessary to get to this very intense state, it's fairly easy to project either outward or inward when you do. Once you're used to this sensation, you'll realize it's not a negative thing; it just means you have an abundance of energy at your command.

The more you meditate and astral project, the more you will probably spontaneously hear and see signs of an astral reality in your day-to-day activities, especially when you're relaxed, because the energy takes a while to fully dissipate. You might start to hear voices, a ringing noise and see flashes of light, NOT indications that you are having mental, ear, or eye problems. Accept this new reality for the blessing it is meant to be, but stay in control. If the distractions become too frequent or too intense, demand out loud that they leave; and they will.

When I haven't astral projected for a while, it takes me usually a few sessions to build up the necessary momentum. There is much more energy available immediately in a very carefully planned group session because we all nourish each other with astral energy all the time. From my experience, it is difficult to relax in these group sessions unless all the members are well known to each other or unless a trusted member stays alert on the physical to supervise the gathering.

Additional Astral Projections

As amazing as it sounds, sometimes we project more than one astral body at a time. I know it sounds crazy; but it is true.

For instance, in your deep trance state you could see a projection of yourself probably flying. You might be discouraged because you are not centered in that energy. And, for me anyway, this was a common occurrence at one time.

There was the part of me who stayed behind to breathe; there was the projection flying in the sky; but there was also the one who observed. It took me a while to realize I had projected two astral bodies and was centered in the observer. I needed to change my focus and the direction of my gaze to have my astral projection adventure. Once I learned to do that, my travels became much more vivid and exciting.

It is also very common to have one or more astral projections but not be centered in the outgoing energy at all but in the energy that stays behind and breathes gently, so you won't have a memory of the experience. You will know when a projection leaves your physical body because you will suddenly become tired and chilled. When it returns, you will become energized, sometimes with a start. People who wake up suddenly in the middle of the night might do so because a projection originating from the dream state has returned.

An experience of mine demonstrates this truth: "The separation was in a whole different manner, I remained in my physical body while I felt energy projecting away from me in continuous waves. I became a being of white light energized by my heart chakra."

Air Quality

An important consideration is the quality of the air you will be breathing very deeply. You need a good supply of healthy oxygen.

In this day and age, we are taught that to conserve the heat in a house we must seal the windows, doors and attic so that heat does not escape. The problem here is that we end up breathing the same air over and over. I suggest you open your windows some time during the day and let the fresh air circulate throughout your home. It stands to reason that you will be healthier and deep breathing for meditation will be more effective.

We are all connected to each other on this planet very intimately by the exchange of atoms found in the air we breathe. On the astral and higher levels, these atoms retain our essence and that of all others they have thus touched. By using highly spiritual meditation, we can elevate the vibrations of these atoms we breathe and thus bless all others who later breathe them. The wind can spread wonderful light and happiness or gloom; it's our choice.

Yoga

Yoga is a spiritual practice that originated in India and designed to assist in holy meditation.

The ancient yogis considered astral projection to be a distraction from their goal of self-enlightenment. The combination of meditation, deep breathing, and stretching exercises of yoga sometimes brings on these experiences.

The yoga headstand in particular is known for opening the crown chakra, which is a primary exit point and located just over the very top of the head. If you don't feel you're flexible enough to do it, even the preparation for it is very valuable. There are many excellent yoga instruction books on the market that give detailed guidance.

If this is out of the question, consider lying on your back on a bed and then lowering your head and your upper body over the edge. Use common sense. If you're elderly, sickly, or your health-care professional or your own inner guidance advises against it, don't do it. There are lots of other ways to prepare.

The Yoga sun-piercing breath is practiced by some to help with astral projection. I've used it many years ago and with success. However, eventually it leaves a red mark in the middle of the forehead caused by the breaking of blood vessels and takes many years to heal and fade. This marking is a sacred symbol in India.

Confidence Building

If you want your confidence to build and need some kind of physical proof that you can do astral projection, do the following: On a day when there is no wind and there are white, puffy stationary clouds in the sky, if you stare at one point in such a cloud for a minute or two, a hole will always form. At first you will think it is just a coincidence and you might have to try it again. Here is evidence that you can send your energy, a part of you, all the way up to the clouds.

As you stare at the cloud, imagine how it would feel to be floating inside it. Try to smell and feel the moisture and look out through its fog. The more you do this, the more real your visit will become. It's a good way to start because astral projection in and out of clouds can eventually be used as a bridge to other realities.

You can project your hands most easily because we use them to express emotions. In the physical, start by stretching, massaging, and blowing on them. Make believe you have a beach ball. Think of what it would feel like to hold it and toss it up and down. You could also clap your pretend hands. You'll be amazed at how real your pretend hands will feel in no time at all.

Destination

Stick to one general type of trip at a time so you don't get fragmented, but don't get too specific. Trust your guides to have the final say. For instance, don't request to go to your last lifetime on Earth because for all you know you might have been a miscarriage. And remember you're on the time schedule of your guides.

If you don't have a destination in mind at the very first stages of your astral projection, sometimes you'll be back inside the physical faster than you want; other times I have found I can fly instead and experience tremendous freedom.

Sometimes foggy-looking clouds appear on the screen my closed eyelids make and interfere with my plans. They must be either ignored or shaped into the destination. They respond to commands and will bring your destination to you and then you enter it.

Chanting (explained later) will help to clear and shape the clouds. You can change the clouds into your tunnel (also explained later) and your destination will appear in the center.

Natural Ability

Music, such as Gregorian chant, may increase your natural ability for astral projection, but unless you want it as a controlling influence, only play it during your preparation routine.

Imagine what any image looks like from the opposite side and then from the top. If you have chosen a tree, ask yourself what the other side looks like and then what it looks like from the sky looking downward. Don't be concerned with accuracy; just start to get a feeling for being outside of your body.

When very relaxed, imagine you can pass your hand through an object or jump off the side of a mountain.

To make an astral projection more intense practice visualizing one or more rainbow colors or brilliant white light and then add shape and movement. Visualization is the tool that will move the intensity of a projection up the scale. When you are high on the scale, there will be no doubt; you will know the difference between imagination and astral projection. You will say to yourself, "Something happened; this is real."

Twirling

In the higher realms energy flows in a circular movement; so a good daily preparation is twirling; about 20 spins will help to loosen your physical attachment. The goal is not to twirl until you get so dizzy that you fall on the floor and then project; that's not what I recommend. However, doing controlled spinning either clockwise or counterclockwise before an astral projection attempt is very valuable. Spinning should be done in your bare feet and using common sense.

Advanced: With your arms held straight forming right angles to your body, palms facing downward, head held high, rotate on the ball of one foot; take small circular steps with the other. Your speed should always be comfortable.

Intermediate: To reduce dizziness as you twirl, clasp your hands together so that you can stare at your thumbnails.

Beginner: Slowly walk in a circle, arms at your side.

Make sure there is no furniture with sharp edges near and that there's a soft resting place close by.

Positions

In order to help control your mind, the real important thing is to keep your back comfortably straight and your mouth closed except while chanting the AUM as I will explain later.

The yoga sitting postures were designed to meditate with a straight back, a great idea if you're a yogi adept. It's also possible to do astral projection from a sitting position using a fairly comfortable chair with extra cushioned support to help you maintain a straight back. From a lying-down position (which I prefer and think is easier), it is best to be on a very firm mattress or futon, lying straight on your back, no pillow, no distractions, with your head pointing to the north.

Compasses work because there is an energy pull from the south to the north. If you put a blade of grass in a wide cup of water, placed on a level surface, the grass will move to the north/south axis. You can use this energy flow to your advantage to help you project from the lying-down position.

If you have long hair, pull it gently so that you feel a slight pressure on your scalp. If you have short hair, place a pillow not under your head but positioned so that you can feel a gentle pressure on the very top of your head. This helps open your crown chakra, a common exit point.

Rays of Light and Energy

If you meditate on the colors blood red, black, brown, gray, or beige, they will only bring you to a lower astral state. Use brilliant shades of vibrant rainbow colors and white in a circular movement instead.

It sometimes starts quite simply in the imagination and then progresses to more real experiences. Do not get discouraged because it will happen quite naturally as you build up a momentum of energy.

There are teachings, in which I believe, that we came into this life on one or more beautiful-colored rays of light and energy and that it stays with us. Try meditating on rainbow colors and white one at a time and you will know which one (or maybe more than one) is your ray. It will be the most easy for you to visualize; you will feel electricity pumping through your body; and it will be the color(s) that makes you the most happy. Meditating on it can act as a pathway out as well as inward.

Feeling Secure

Choose a quiet, comfortable, dimly lit, neat and secure place. You have probably spent many lifetimes sleeping around an open fire or huddled in a cave where for survival you needed to be fully awake at the slightest disturbance. Your subconscious mind remembers and needs to feel very secure to relax. If you are trying to have an astral projection from the center of a large, fairly empty room, it's probably not going to work as well as if you're in a smaller more cozy setting. Make sure it is quiet, doors are closed and there are no edges of furniture pointing at you nor should you be under exposed ceiling beams. This advice might not make mental sense, but it makes emotional sense.

When you have your astral projection, the part of you that is left behind will experience a chill needing extra warmth and comfort, perhaps a blanket, but one that does not contain wool is best, because you don't want to pick up on the energies of animals.

Distractions

Because of a charge of healthy energy flow, your physical body could experience some twitching and itching. Deep meditation can also become a diuretic. In other words, expect distractions; don't be discouraged or try to ignore them; that's just how it works in the beginning especially.

You start wherever you are:

If you are distracted by tension, it can be released by visualizing the color violet entering your body on the in-breath. If you take a calcium and/or mineral supplement anyway, consider taking it just before your astral projection attempt.

If you are distracted by physical pain, meditate on it frequently and offer it up to God. Mentally turn it also into violet-colored light. From my experience, your pain will then either dissolve or move and can be chased. The more you chase it, the weaker it becomes. And, most amazingly, your health will start to improve or an avenue that leads to good health will open up. And I'm not even remotely suggesting that you don't also deal with physical pain or ill health as your health-care provider suggests.

If you are distracted by emotional pain, visualize the problem or condition above your head and offer it to your higher energies to heal. The problem or your attitude towards it will then start to improve.

If you are distracted by anger or other negativity coming to you from other people, when you are alone, out loud talk to them. Call them by name and extend love and respect. Express your gratitude for their presence. If it's very difficult to show love, remember they are also part of God's creation and imagine them as they once were as young children. You will be amazed that they will pick up on this energy and their attitude towards you will improve.

If you are distracted by rumbling noise and motion in your belly, you might have a parasite problem in your digestive tract. You could eat lots of ground-up, raw, fresh ginger, raw garlic or the ground-up herb turmeric especially first thing in the morning for cleansing. Please check with your health-care provider first. It could also be just a noise and feeling that your digestive tract is moving along.

If you are distracted because you are sick, tired, or depressed, one thing you can do is meditate on a pine tree. Mentally embrace it; feel its energy and life force enter your body. Live in the present moment with it. Experience its love for All That Is. The problem here is that you will become energized and start to think of more mundane things that you "just have to get up and do right away."

This deep state of meditation is also self-induced hypnosis. If you have any personal changes to your behavior you desire to make, this is the time to assert the positive, just be careful and plan ahead. My warning is that I believe I have brought on spells of nausea by telling myself over and over that I dislike certain foods. I went too far. There's a delicate balance to maintain here.

Your True Identity

Pause for a moment and experience your true identity, not as a human but as a sphere of life located between your eyes, not even inside your body, but attached through tension just outside. Release the tension and you have the freedom to come and go as you please. I suggest you meditate for a time on your true self and its location so that you will more fully realize that you are already separate from your physical.

Think about it. You do one of two things. If you move a physical part of you, your attention will first travel inside your body for a tiny fraction of a second to that part of you that will be moved. You'll need to flex some muscles. After all, that's how your physical body is designed. However, if you only think of a part of your physical body with no intention of movement, your attention doesn't travel through your body; it travels for a brief, short moment on the outside. SURPRISE! SURPRISE! You do astral projection all the time. And notice also that it's only part of you that travels to your foot, your hand, or wherever. Most of you stays located between your eyes and you also continue to breathe. This is exactly how projection really works, no hocus pocus involved. It's part of how we operate all the time.

Please take the time to digest and experiment a bit with what I've just explained. It's imperative that you understand before you proceed.

Sphere of Light

Even though it is certainly possible to exit from any point within your body, when using my techniques, you will probably exit through your head or the very center of your chest so a gentle massage of those areas would be helpful. Loosen or remove any tight or restricting clothing.

Raise your physical arms above your head. Close your eyes. Think of the space between your hands as a sphere of your favorite colored, positive light. Let the sphere remain above your head as you return your physical hands to your lap or your side.

Pay attention to the sphere. Show your creation love by extending imaginary hands up to it and pretend to caress and kiss it. Let the sphere of light remain above your head not only in meditation but throughout your day. (My days go much easier when I follow my own advice here.) The more you meditate on and enjoy it, the more vivid it will become and the easier it will be for your guides to contact you and the more frequent and real your astral projections will be.

Tunnels

There are energies with us always that on the astral plane appear as tunnels connecting us to our past, future, and other realities. People who have near-death visions see and sometimes travel through one leading to the other side.

If you stare at a sheet of plain, white paper or a white wall, pretty soon you will see a small, vibrating, colored sphere of light, maybe surrounded by the appearance of a tunnel or even some circular lines. It might be necessary to raise your chin and lower but not shut your eyes. This is the energy you are sending out which combines with your karma, words, thoughts, astrological, and numerological energies and forms the events and emotions that make up your life.

You project to whatever holds your attention all the time. Life is the act of projecting and then experiencing. After all, we are here to learn. You project even while asleep and call it dreaming.

With your eyes closed, for a couple of minutes, VERY LIGHTLY massage in a circular motion first in one direction then the other the back of your head, the area at the base of the skull and just above the neck. Doing so will help you start to see at least one tunnel which could be rotating in either direction. It sometimes helps to move your closed eyes in a circular movement first one way then the other or very gently massage your forehead in a circular direction.

If you stare in a very relaxed manner with closed eyes in the very center of the screen your closed eyelids make, the tunnel and sometimes the vibrating light in the center will then appear. Sometimes you will just see a few circular lines and that's okay. If you're at a crossroads in your life, you could see the outline of two or more tunnels.

Make the tunnel more intense by moving your closed eyes in fast circles, either direction works for me. Pay close attention to the center of your tunnel and look for movement. This is where your astral projections will start.

You can be anywhere you desire. The trick is to pay very close attention to the center of the screen your closed eyelids make, where the center of your tunnel is whether you can see it or not, and where the movement will start. The more you focus there, the faster it will happen. Just think of it and your tunnel will take you. Do it. It's life altering.

Common sense dictates that massaging a soft place on your head should be done with caution. Please do not be tempted to put a vibrator on the area or apply any pressure. It's just a very light touching. You won't intensify your experience by harming your head. Be careful.

Chanting

In the ancient Sanskrit language, one of the sacred names for God is AUM, also spelled OM It is believed by some to be the sound of God in the process of creation. Inhaling deeply then chanting and singing it on the exhale will give energy and bring a higher plane of vibration. I find it releases tension, brings a feeling of peace and holiness, and helps me control my mind. The more you deep breathe, the more relaxed you will become. Tightness you might not have realized you had can be detected and released; it's what keeps us attached to the physical. After a while, your breath will naturally slow down and you will have your astral projection adventure. With some people when their bodies need more oxygen, it will wake them up and, to continue their travels, they deep breathe until their bodies slow their breath down again. Such healthy breathing becomes effortless. With others, like myself, I just forget about my physical body and it takes care of itself as when asleep.

From a sitting position it's easier. AUM and the work "home" sound the same except for the letter "h"; there is the hard "O" sound and then a long humming of the letter "m". It's a disgrace that this sacred sound is sometimes the object of jokes. I hope you don't let that deter you.

Inhale deeply through your nose with your mouth closed; as you exhale sing one long AUM at whatever pitch. There should be longer and longer pauses on the out breath. It's a breathing technique as well as a calling out to God. If this is not easy for you to do, it's probably because your breath needs to be deeper.

The screen your closed eyelids make changes instantly. You will see round-shaped energies that appear alive. Look for a tunnel to start to form on the screen your closed eyelids make.

Sacred Color

The following is my belief in the meaning of the rainbow-colored rays of light. The origin of most of my understanding originated with a now-defunct offshoot church of the St Germaine Foundation, one from the Buddhists (the color tangerine) and the meaning of the merging of the three primary colors into white (as far as I know) is my personal belief.

The color pink represents the female aspect of the God Flame--love for All That Is. Blue is the male side--the power to accomplish the positive and to overcome the negative. Gold is the offspring--wisdom. Together these three rays become the Holy Trinity. The merging of the three into the one, the white, the power of innocence, is the One True God. The combination of only two of the rays: Green is prosperity and good health. Tangerine is enlightenment. Violet is forgiveness and mercy.

I have further been instructed and believe that when one color is present, they are all there even though they might not be visible. It makes no difference to the Creator if you are male or female.

Each one has an important and unique role to play which is now beyond our comprehension. We would not even exist if we did not all have an abundance of each color. We just need to recognize that fact.

I don't mean to infer that if someone cannot see and understand color in the same manner as the rest of us, they cannot do astral projection and have vivid dreams. Every one of us has this ability. We just need to develop our own individual pathway.

Suppose you're color blind, then meditate on any beautiful light you do see. Perhaps you've always been totally blind; a pathway is also there for you. Pray and it will open. Perhaps colors don't look the same to any of us, who knows for sure. Use the tools you do have and guidance will be given.

Chakras

A chakra is a sphere of brilliant color and energy. They give us life itself.

Through visualization and meditation this holy light from our high chakras will increase and become more intense throughout our physical, mental, and emotional worlds. The colors will blend and bring us the power of astral projection from either the waking or the sleeping state, and, as the Buddhists believe, bring us good health and a good life.

Position your attention at your heart chakra, located in the very center of your chest at your backbone. You will know you are in the correct location when you smile. All kinds of tension come and go in all of us especially in this location; otherwise we would not be here on the physical plane. Before you can progress further, it needs to be released. Picture a violet-colored flame, bringing forgiveness and mercy, engulfing and dissolving any negativity.

While visualizing a sphere of rainbow-colored or brilliant white light at your heart chakra, or simply the color rose/pink an overpowering feeling of love will come over you. If you do at least five minutes of deep breathing centered there, you acknowledge the part of you that stays behind and you start the separation.

You might also find the sacred color of gold as well as the pink. Imagine that you can breathe in that location and expand the light to fill your physical body and then the whole universe. With this technique, you will have the energy needed and you will find that no matter where it is you want to have an astral projection, you will already be there. You'll be using your love for your Mother God as your engine.

On the out breath, chant the AUM. If you inhale through your mouth, your mind will wander more easily. Pause after the out breath because you can separate during the pauses. Repeat until you have so much breath in you that your physical body feels numb and heavy. This is how you can start your engine for obe and inner world travel.

There are two problems with this beginning: (1) Energy could take over and you might be tempted to end your meditation and complete some everyday chore instead. (2) An astral projection might come before you're ready and it would probably be out of control, a projection of flying real fast for instance (they are fun).

Deep breathe through your nose while meditating on your throat chakra, colored blue, as the Buddhists teach. This is where you gain control of your astral projection or lucid dream. You will feel your connection with your Father God and have the power to accomplish the positive. Look for movement on the screen your closed eyelids make. If you don't see motion, move your closed eyes in circles.

Since blue is the power of the Godhead, our Father God, who brings the power to overcome the negative and accomplish the positive, it appears to be a lot easier to astral project to a blue object. This is an easy way. The throat chakra, colored blue, I have found to be one of the keys to astral projection. Projecting to a small, simple, blue object can become fairly easy once you meditate first on the color blue at your throat. As I project to the blue object, my fingers immediately feel both sides of its edge. The memory of touch is a very important tool.

Relax and enjoy the moment.

After another five minutes or so work your way up to the very center of your head, another powerful chakra. I see a white sphere covered with gold. Gold brings holiness and wisdom. This is you, the offspring of God; the center white is your connection to the Godhead. You'll find it so powerful you won't want to leave. You will discover your identity as an exceptional, beautiful and unique part of the glorious body of God.

Astral Plane

There is a vibrant world filled with life all around us that is not usually seen nor felt from the physical perspective. It is called the astral plane.

Once you have entered by deep breathing, chanting, and meditation, you will see the astral counterpart of the screen your eyelids form when your eyes are closed. Small forms of etheric matter could play across the screen; with practice you can change them. Faces might come, one right after another—maybe guides or people from previous, future, or parallel lifetimes—and beautiful colored spheres of light.

One of the real secrets to astral projection both inward and outward is right before your eyes. Pay attention to depth, detail and shading on your screen; and don't simply look at it, but stare at it while still relaxed.

Because these mind-boggling adventures mostly happen at the unique moment between waking and sleeping, the best time to make your attempt is when you're tired. It could go one of four ways, all of them good: (1) You might become energized with a feeling of wellness resulting from your meditation but that will probably end your attempt to project. (2) You could start to doze and possibly astral project just before sleep takes over. (3) You could see visions (an astral projection that comes to you). (4) If you go to sleep, you can still astral project from a lucid dream.

There are two things you can do to make the process even easier. Just as you enter a deep meditation or doze off, a powerful action is to affirm your intentions several times out loud, something like: "I AM THAT I AM outside of my body." The second is to visualize a flame of sacred light and mentally place it in the very center of the screen your closed eyes make, right where your astral projection will start.

With patience and determination look for whatever or wherever your destination and it will either come to you or you will go to it.

Vibrations

Vibrations accompany outward astral projections and inner-world experiences. To have frequent and vibrant trips, increase the intensity and frequency of these vibrations by paying attention to them. Don't wait for the vibrations to increase on their own; take control yourself. They sound like a ringing and a little bit like the noise of crickets. The sound is always faintly in your head. As you progress to higher states of consciousness, the ringing (from my experience) will become louder and of a higher pitch. You might hear a popping and a snapping noise.

Visualize brilliant golden, pink, blue and white light, shimmering with rainbow colors, or whatever beautiful colors draw you, filling you with love and opening your path back to All That Is. This technique brings tremendous happiness, a wonderful feeling of wellbeing and lots of healthy energy.

As I've mentioned earlier, occasionally, while in deep meditation, the vibrations might become so intense that you feel paralyzed. It's easy to slip out into an obe at this time, but if you change your mind, you can just relax, move your fingers, mentally say "no", and the vibrations will decrease.

Candle-Flame Gazing

There is one side effect that I have encountered and perhaps you will as well. I'm not sure. Without any effort a rainbow of colors appeared to me around streetlights, the moon, and some other indoor and outdoor lights. They're not bright enough to hamper my vision and are not a problem; they're just beautiful.

Locate yourself inside a cozy small room or separate a larger room into a small area. You need to feel secure. A darkened room, but not necessarily without any light, is best so the light from the candle flame appears more intense and hypnotic.

Be very safety oriented. Candle flames have a long history of starting fires. The candle should not be placed on a windowsill. There should be no curtains, tablecloths, or other flammable objects nearby. Place the candle securely inside the candle holder and locate it in the center of a large flameproof plate. I strongly suggest using unscented candles; otherwise you might be breathing in chemical fumes. When your experience is over, don't leave the flame burning. Following this advice will not only give you safety but peace of mind, very necessary for deep meditation.

As explained previously, make sure your back is as straight as is comfortable for you. Once you're settled pray for assistance from high spiritual guides.

When the candle is first lit, pay close attention to how it appears, because later when you are seeing it on the astral you will want to remember for comparison's sake.

There will be rays of light that seem to travel from the flame to our eyes and back. I believe that is a reflection of the physical light onto our eyeballs because when my eyes move, the rays move as well.

Next I simply gaze directly into the flame. Gaze and gaze until you become the flame. There will be light extending from the flame like an aura, and you'll feel unconditional love flowing from the flame. You'll understand why fire was worshiped by many tribes in prehistoric times.

Breathe its light into the center of your head if your goal is to project from the waking state. Breathe its light into the center of your throat if your goal is to project later from the sleeping state. It's efficient to do both, one at a time. Once that's established, let this amazing holy energy extend from you and flood all life everywhere. As you gaze longer and longer, you will find part of yourself in the flame and everyone and everything that you love; it becomes unconditional love itself.

You'll know when you're in the astral because then the air has motion and becomes alive. The flame of your candle will have a beautiful golden colored sphere of energy surrounded by a rose color, even to the point of a rainbow further out. Relax and let it happen. Don't be discouraged; be persistent. If need be, do it day after day until you succeed. Such meditation once a week might not work for you. I suggest daily gazing. Each time you start to gaze you'll wonder why you ever stopped.

Projecting Inward

When you meditate on your heart chakra, you will experience who and what you really are, a spiritual being of great love and light. Whatever is going on in your physical life will suddenly have little or no meaning. There will only be the present moment filled with tremendous love and strength. This becomes an awesome inner projection that can be turned into a healing time by mentally expanding this wonderful light and energy to fill your entire body. This energy is God given to each of us at conception and then maintained by God throughout our lives. By acknowledging its presence we can heal not only ourselves but those around us.

Another way to get inside for an inner world experience is to gently focus your attention at the center of your head, where a powerful chakra is also located. Mentally color it a beautiful rainbow color. I use a white sphere surrounded by gold. Get used to the feeling of movement by going back and forth from your heart chakra to your head chakra. This is how you project, by moving your attention because you are wherever your attention is.

Projecting Outward

To turn this wondrous experience into an astral projection outward, pretend your heart chakra expands and becomes a beautiful cloud-shaped space above your body. The more you meditate on it, the more centered you will be in it and the more real it becomes. You will then quietly float above your body.

Another way: relax and deep breathe with your attention traveling from the top of your head to the bottom of your feet, in unison with your breath. You'll find you will naturally travel on top of your body not inside. Pay attention to the sound of the ringing in your ears. Let it get louder and ever louder. You'll have the feeling that you're floating in a soft, white cloud. It happens in a very matter-of-fact manner. Feel intense love for all.

To make it easier, meditate on the freedom and happiness such an astral projection will bring you. You'll be in the astral realm and emotion reigns supreme there. There will be the one who stays behind and slowly and quietly breathes and the one who floats above. You will be filled with tremendous energy and love.

Pretend you can do it and then you will. If you have problems it's because there is doubt which brings tension. Dissolve the tension away by meditating on the color violet. It will be as easy as you allow it to be.

You say you try and try but can't travel on top of your body? Keep in mind you do it all the time. Bear with me. To make this experience very real, start by raising your knees and vigorously rubbing them. Work with the sensation of feeling. Perhaps put your favorite perfume on them so you can use your sense of smell. Lay on your back with your knees bent upward, feet firmly on your mattress. On the inhale, think about your knees, on your exhale think about the top of your head. You won't be inside your physical body unless you choose to be. You'll be on top of your body going back and forth. Do this over and over until you feel the need to lower your legs.

Continue only now travel from your head to the point where your knees used to be. After a while, let your breathing slow way down and so also will the time it takes to travel back and forth. You will feel lighter and a tingling sensation. You'll hear a ringing in your ears. Intensify these feelings through practice and your attention to them. Continue going back and forth until you realize that you are experiencing an astral projection with ease.

When you are so filled with oxygen that your breath naturally pauses for a moment, center your attention very intensely in midair. In deep meditation you can focus on any point you choose with very little effort. And expect the point of your focus to slowly drift upward as you continue to breathe softly. Relax and go with it.

Now you have changed the direction of your travels. Instead of going from your head to your knees, you are going from your physical body upward. In C. Lorraine LeBlanc's wonderful book, "Stumbling Upon the Spiritual Path" in Chapter One, she explains. A very small part of us is actually located inside the physical body. Our presence, our energy and light, is really a huge sphere extending way beyond our physical manifestation. You see, a large part of you is already outside all the time. Think about the area above you and you'll be there. There should be almost no effort when very relaxed.

Projecting Upward

In the teachings of Beloved Saint Germaine, we learn that the space above our head is where our Higher Mental Body dwells, above that is our Mighty I AM Presence. The Hindus teach that this space above us is a second heart chakra. Jim Hertack in his book "The Keys of Enoch" (Academy for Future Science, 2007) talks about two chakras located above the head. When you give yourself permission to contact God directly, you're apt to smile and raise your arms above your head. So there are many arrows pointing to this space as being very sacred and powerful. Meditating on it as beautiful light and energy is a most wondrous experience and an easy way out.

This technique works best if done immediately following astral projection from the heart chakra (as already discussed, floating on top of your body). You will already be centered in a ball of love energy that will follow your focus and commands and will bring you upward.

Think of going to an astral counterpart of outer space; make the request out loud. Remember what the sky looks like at evening time in the country, just filled with stars. Stare very intensely (while still very relaxed) at the center of the screen your closed eyelids make looking for a single beautiful star. This point will become the center of a tunnel pointing upward. You will then see wondrous flashes of twinkling light. The longer you stay focused, the more vivid they become.

If you don't have a feeling of movement, to travel upward, motion with your projected arms in the opposite direction that you would swim using the breaststroke. To project your arms, just pretend. The feeling of love will be your engine. As you move forward, using the power of loving All That Is, bring outer space within and you will travel massive amounts of space in a short time. You can fly with the angelic host if you choose.

Once you arrive at your own higher energy, you will feel complete.

Our True Identity

Acknowledge where you are located most of the time, right between your eyes, not even inside your body but on the edge of it. If you pause and think about it, you will recognize this statement as the truth. Believe that you are already a separate entity from your physical body, its function being that of a vehicle. For additional support of this belief, I offer the following:

Swami Muktananda, in the second edition of his book "Meditate" (Copyright 1980, 1991, SYDA Foundation) talks about the benefit of even once seeing the Self as separate from the physical body.

A.D.K. Luk in the book the "Law of Life", Book One (Copyright 1959, A. D. K. Luk Publications) explains that we are not a physical body but a stream of light, a projected ray from the Godhead.

In Paul Williams book, "Remember Your Essence" (Copyright, 1987, Harmony Books) he compares our true self to an ever-burning log of wood and the fire to our life force.

In the wonderful book, "Stumbling Upon The Spiritual Path", (Self-Published, Copyright 2006, available at Amazon), C. Lorraine LeBlanc channels her individual manifestation of God. She explains that as we grow we become aware of consciousness of which we are a part in physical reality.

Master Subramuniya expressed it very well in "The Self God" (original Copyright 1959; 10th edition, copyright 1973, Comstock House). He explains that we are light in an illusion created by ourselves.

Paramahansa Yogananda in "How You Can Talk with God" (Copyright 1957 & 1985, Self-Realization Fellowship). He explains the energy we all feel that operates our physical manifestation.

Are you stuck? Are you not keeping up? Relax about it and let's take a side trip.

As described above, lay on your back, bring your attention to the very center of your chest. Breathe very deeply through your nose until you hear intense ringing in your ears and you feel heavy. That part you can do. It just takes some time and focus. Pretend you're five-years old. Clap your pretend hands until you know they are your projected hands. Move your pretend feet up and down until you know they are your projected feet. Do this for a few minutes.

Now give yourself a real treat. With your projected hands, massage your physical feet. Trust me, it's easy. This will help you relax deeper and deeper. Do this until your projected feet float in a white cloud above your body.

Once you know you can float your feet, it gives you tremendous confidence that the rest of your astral body will follow. Massage your back with your projected (or pretend) hands and, most important of all, massage the area between your eyes. Do this relaxation technique until you're out, however long it might take, however many sessions it might take. IT WORKS. It's worth the effort. It will change you forever.

Having said all the above, you could instead take a shortcut!! Unless you choose to, for the wonderful experience it is, you don't need to project or float an entire replica of your physical body. The only part you really need to project is the energy that is really you, located between your eyes. Start out by massaging your head with your projected hands, then the area between your eyes, separate from the tension there and you're out. Make it even easier by visualizing that sphere as holy, amazingly beautiful light. Make it energy you will enjoy melting into.

PART TWO, INSTRUCTIONS

My Techniques

Even astral projections that are centered close to the physical world there will be no sensation of feeling or smelling unless you bring it with you. If you do it will make your astral trips much more intense.

Decide where it is you want to go. What places do you love the most? Do you love the ocean? The forest? A time in the past? Wherever that is for you, make that your first trip. If it's the ocean, remember the sensation and smell of the water and the waves moving. If it's a forest, remember what it's like to climb a tree; remember the feeling of the branches and the leaves. If it's a time in the past, I have found time to be an illusion. You can go there, just recall and concentrate on something from the physical you vividly remember that was there. If these places have a strong, positive emotional attachment, that memory will help as well.

I like to feel the hand of an angel or spiritual guide that is helping me. Feel a hand pulling you upward.

Everyone can do this and you're no exception. You'll find your own unique pathway and I can help.

Two Methods to Project to Wooded Areas

The First Method

I'm putting this technique first because it is the easier of the two and you can build on it later. Of all my astral projection techniques, it's one of the simplest and most basic.

People who garden a lot and love to do it frequently have an astral projection to their gardens when they take a nap or retire for the evening. They can't help it. They don't know how they do it; they just do it. You can also quite easily use this same pull of Nature. It can become a very valuable tool. You'll find tremendous holy energy there available for astral projection. When out for a walk in a wooded area pay close attention to the trees and other plants. Absorb their holy energy. Touch the trunks, branches and leaves of the trees. While walking imagine yourself flying above and through the trees. Imagine what the wind would feel like. Then look upward and study the sky and the clouds. Stay long enough to experience a kinship of love with Nature. During your attempts, use all of your senses. Remember what it feels like to touch a branch, what it would smell like especially if you choose a pine tree, and what the sense of total freedom that flying in the sky with no fear of falling would bring you. You could also gaze at Nature through a window, or indoors at a potted plant. This memory will be very valuable later. The easiest places to have an astral projection and dream about will be related to wherever your attention has most recently been placed. If that is Nature, you have a heads up. Flying through the woods is a most awesome adventure.

After completing your preparation, as previously described, place your memory right between your eyes until Nature appears. You can enter your vision by remembering the sense of touch and smell as previously described. You will then feel motion and travel to places where the plants and trees grow.

Meditate on the screen your closed eyelids make. Once you see at least a few circular lines, look to the bottom and probably to the left of your screen. Request to go to a wooded area. Expect to see trees moving toward you; but if you don't or if your vision of them is very faint, repeat your request to your tunnel. Have patience and they will then appear. If you have the experience of flying either over or through different colors of light instead, it's because you are not close to the physical but higher up in the astral or etheric plane. You can get closer to the physical by simply making the request to your tunnel.

If you want to fly, I suggest you think of the tops of trees and you'll see them forming at the bottom and sides of your tunnel. You'll have the feeling of flying through the sky, probably out of control. One way to gain command is to remember what a cool breeze feels like. You can change your direction by turning your gaze. You can stop by looking directly at something. In the beginning this might be easier said than done, but with practice you will succeed. It's very important at this stage to think of where it is you want to go. Use visualization, the memory of touch and smell. To succeed, be very happy.

This first method starts out usually by being in two places at once. The part of you who stays behind and breathes gently watches the astral projection. The part of you who projects has the feeling of flying over a wooded area, and sometimes there will be houses, people and animals. It's a very healing, exhilarating and wondrous adventure. It's like watching a 3D movie only you can move inside. To enter your astral projection remember what the wind feels like; with your pretend hands touch the tops of the trees. Very surprisingly, you will have the experience of flying above a wooded area. Your every command to your tunnel will be followed. Mentally ask to see the trees more clearly and your trip will slow down and you will see more detail. It's a lot of fun to fly through the trees.

When you are in the air and you feel like you are flying, you might not be. It took me a long time to realize that I was really located in a point in the sky. I had no physical body so I was not subject to gravity. However, the Earth was rotating on its axis. I just had the sensation of moving. It's like when you're in a carwash seated in your automobile. The big brushes come forward and you have the sensation of moving even though you are not.

Sometimes traveling is the obe destination; it is a lot of fun and very rewarding to fly above or through Nature. The more you practice, the more real and easier it will become.

It's as simple as that. Focus and repeat daily until it works for you. You will have success. You'll be able to use Nature as a launching pad to spring from one reality to another. It will even make it much easier to reach the heaven worlds. Throughout your day, pause and think about how it would be if you were swinging from a tree branch like a monkey and then to fly.

Don't be surprised if a holy guide interrupts and takes you on another type of trip. Sometimes it's a good idea to just go wherever your guides lead you. There's always a reason for every trip.

The Second Method

As in the previous technique, we can all use Nature as a portal to exciting astral projection experiences. To prepare, go out for a walk someplace you find especially beautiful and peaceful. Imagine you can fly over the landscape on your walk only much slower and closer to the ground than the previous technique. Touch and smell as much as possible. Meditate there until you feel an overwhelming love for all. Get very intense; pretend that your eyes can photograph the scene as you walk along. Choose an object to take home such as a wild flower, a rock, a leaf or a small branch of a tree.

You can spend hours looking at Nature and nothing will happen until you pay attention to detail, shading, and depth. Then you will be flooded with love which is the fuel for astral projections and inner world travel.

Later when you are at home, place the object you have brought with you on a table near a comfortable chair or you can simply gaze at an object of Nature through a window. Your back should be straight. Deep breathe and chant the AUM until you are in the trance state. Stare at your object until you feel that overwhelming sense of unconditional love. It should remind you of a time as a child when you were loved not for anything you did or said but just because you existed.

Gaze especially at details. Once this love relationship is established, close your eyes and you will see at least a small flicker of the object on the screen your eyelids make when they are closed. Ask your tunnel to take you to other places where it also exists. And it will. Pay close attention to details and it will appear clearer. Tell it to expand and you will see the whole object, not the one you're meditating on but another one in the wild. Ask for more to appear and they will. Your first thought might be that it's an optical illusion. Just let that thought come and go, but work with the image. Command it to come closer, become more vivid, turn, grow, and multiply. Amazingly, your directions will be followed and you will be in a clearing in a wooded area. Have patience and make as many attempts at this as you need until your astral projection is as vibrant and as clear as you want it to be. Listen for the ringing in your ears.

You will experience what you expect. Be sure to make it a bright sunny day. Never travel to a dark place.

Ask your tunnel for movement. Look for something abundant and close to the ground like dandelions or rabbits. Use your memory of touch and smell as tools. You will have access to many projected hands at the same time. Smell and caress whatever you find. You'll be able to examine the trees especially in layers by traveling through them. Play in nature as though you are a four-year-old. The feeling of petting a rabbit helps me.

If your mind wanders and you lose the image, open your eyes and gaze at the object again. Don't get discouraged, the more the effort, the greater the gain.

If you want to experience a full-body astral projection, this is the perfect technique for you. In your astral projection, look for a pine tree. Give it a full-bodied embrace. Feel its quietness, holiness and power of existing in the moment. Show it love. Feel your entire projected body the size and dimension it is in the physical. And you have it.

The Third Eye

First, if you center your attention at the bridge of your nose and then fall back to the very center of your head, you will be able to locate an astral eye and use it. Amazingly, if you request it, the screen your closed eyelids make will move to the top of your head because this "eye" will be awakened and functioning.

You might have the sensation of passing through a tunnel. It happens in a very matter-of-fact manner. You can then have an astral projection through your crown chakra located just above the very top of your head by simply focusing on the center of your screen and thinking of doing it.

I suggest your goal should be to project your eyes and the space between your eyes because the easiest form to project is a sphere of emotional light containing your eyes. You need to have a destination planned or your trip might end sooner than you want. It's a good method to fly over vast landscapes or the ocean. You'll have the sensation of experiencing tremendous freedom.

As explained earlier, after following the above instructions, you might instead see spheres of beautiful light. If this happens, you'll know that even though you might not have separated yet, you are on a high astral plane. Expect to hear a ringing and sometimes a popping noise. Pay attention to these noises and lights so they will increase; they accompany a lot of astral projections and inner-world experiences.

The more you practice this technique, the easier it becomes, to the point that it is among the simplest and most direct methods for astral projection.

Two Ways to Contact Your Holy Guides

The First Method

Out loud request one or more of your guides to be kind enough to present themselves. Their visit might happen during the following astral projection attempt or later during a dream or as you awaken in the morning. The timing will be a decision of your guides.

Blow on and rub and massage your hands. If in a sitting position, raise your arms above your head, if lying down to the north of your head. Keep them there for as long as your arm muscles will allow. Return your hands to your lap or to your side but do not mentally move the space that was between your hands. Fill it with a rainbow color or brilliant white letting it become a sphere of light. When the visualization is firmly set, see it move. As it moves, you might see it take the form of a holy guide who might offer his/her hand. If that happens, you could project a hand and grasp it, paying attention to the feeling of holding a hand. The more you practice, the more real and sacred your projection will become.

To make your astral projection even more intense, visualize a golden chalice filled with light. Let your guide give you Holy Communion. Feel the chalice with a projected hand especially just inside and outside of the rim and the stem.

The Second Method You may contact the deceased, your higher self, your guides, the angelic host, and all kinds of high beings of light. Pray first that they will be gracious enough to present themselves.

Focus in the very center of your head. At the same time, pay attention to the astral counterpart of the screen your closed eyelids make and direct the screen to also move inward. It will. At first it might not stay for more than a moment, but keep working with it and it will stay longer and longer. Then look not especially for the tunnel but for the light in the center of the tunnel for that is where your guides will appear. Look for and then pay attention to rainbow color or brilliant white light, movement, shading, depth, and detail. Ask for clarity and you will amazingly receive it. Become as determined as necessary and you will be most blessed with their visitations.

Lucid Dreaming, Updated August 2014

Lucid dreams are really inner-world projections that may or may not turn into full astral projections. You can have spectacular adventures this way. Sometimes it takes great determination, sometimes it just happens. To have them, before dozing off to sleep, state out loud the type of dream you wish or even a destination, and ask to remember it. The more spiritual or health-oriented your request, the easier it will be. Presume a guide is there to help and talk to him/her. Be sure to express your gratitude.

As in other methods of astral projection, I suggest you start by meditating at the very center of your chest, your heart chakra. Color it a rosy pink and you will feel the love for All That Is from your Mother God. This will give you the necessary energy.

Next, settle your attention in the very center of your throat chakra, colored blue. Meditating while centering your focus there is a basic pathway to lucid dreaming taught by the Buddhists.

As you meditate on the color blue and centered in your throat, you will start to see other colors and movement which will be the start of your lucid dream. Pay attention and choose your location and goal. If your dream turns into a nightmare, take control of it by saying the word "no." Look for beautiful light. If that doesn't work, move your fingers and toes to wake up.

Just as with astral projection approached from the waking state, an easy way to be in control of your dreams and thus turn them into astral projections is by using the memory of touch. Just before you sleep, think of something you can hold onto throughout your lucid dream like a branch of a tree or simply a stick, something you can get your dream hands around and carry throughout your lucid dream. It has to be something you can strongly remember what a firm grip of it would be. This is one of the ways I change an ordinary dream into one that's vivid and where I have some degree of control.

To be in charge of a dream, you must be able to move about. In one of my recent dreams, there was a bunch of carrots and to gain some control I picked one up and ate it. The memory of how that would feel in the physical helped me a lot. With much determination, you can start by doing such simple things.

You can walk, crawl or (my favorite) dance when dreaming if you first decide to before sleep takes over. Progress at your own pace to jumping possibly even into the clouds and then floating down to the experience of your choice like a former, future, or alternate lifetime. Do it. It's amazing.

You can get issues resolved by asking questions out loud before you retire. Ask the same question night after night until you are very sure of the correct path to take.

I suggest you lay on a very hard mattress or a futon, positioned so that your head is to the north. Lay on your back with no pillow. Close your eyes and intensely gaze at one point on the screen your closed eyelids make. With all your might, stay awake as long as you can. From my experience, the harder I try to stay awake the faster and easier sleep comes.

Follow these instructions every night and the momentum of energy will build up and you will have many adventures and receive much wisdom.

Sometimes after a long, unsuccessful session of astral projection using other methods, stop trying to project and just go to sleep. Because of the large momentum of energy you've probably built up, you'll be able to project quite easily from the sleeping state into a lucid dream.

Pretend you're five-years old and clap or rub your pretend hands. After your tunnel starts to become visible, in the very center of it visualize a wooden or metal bar, something you can remember the feeling of getting your hands around and then carry it throughout your projection. Pretend walking and running will also help. What works for me a lot is the memory of the feeling of brushing up against trees. Your memory of touch can be very valuable.

Be careful. There are trickster spirits out there who might enter your dream time. It's happened to me. To prevent them from entering, meditate on beautiful-colored light and chant the AUM (even silently).

The easiest type of dream to have will be based on the activities of the days recently experienced and on the days of your near future. Yes, I wrote "future." You see, time is really an illusion we have created to experience our life in an orderly manner. When you get into dream time, you can step out of that illusion. To take what I have just said a step further, if you can control your dreams, then you can control parts of your life more easily.

Spectacular adventures are awaiting but you need to remember them. I suggest you get into the habit of reviewing them out loud as you wake and then writing them down immediately. Otherwise you might forget within about 15 seconds.

Then there's also the question of dream interpretation. I believe that if you get all caught up in that pathway, your dreams will become more complex, because you dream what you expect. Aim for clear, concise dreams, refined to your understanding and that's what will happen for you. Expect such things as lessons in life, predictions for your future, guidance from high, spiritual guides, visits from those who have gone to the other side, and, of course, astral projections in a very wide range.

Projecting to a Body of Water

One of the places I like to go is to the ocean. Flying over and through the waves and diving deep within is just wonderful and very strengthening. Look for your tunnel and ask it to take you to the ocean. I find the waves start to appear at the bottom of the screen my closed eyelids make.

Try to use all your senses; remember what the ocean smells, feels and looks like. Visualize things like seaweed, clams, lobster, and fish. Pretend to swim until the experience becomes as real as you choose it to be. Of course, the more you do it, the more vivid it becomes. It's very powerful and healing.

You can enter the consciousness of one of the fish, if you want; but then it will be hard to eat fish later. If you do enter, you will be amazed that you can relate to their emotions and you will find that they also have thoughts and goals.

One evening I picked up on the energy of a fish I had eaten that day. Its last thought before being caught was that if it could just make it to a certain point in the ocean it would be safe and happy. Boy, I sure felt guilty.

Contacting Other Life in Outer Space

Stare at a point in the sky for a few minutes. As I've mentioned before, staring at anything is a projection whether you're centered in it or not. Send out unconditional love. Your energy could be answered in some way either immediately or within a day or sometimes a week or two, either by a vivid dream or an astral projection in the morning as you awaken. A response that I have received is of strong surprise and curiosity.

However, this is one area where great caution should be exercised. In answer to one of my attempts at contact, I received a clear vision containing many squares, triangles, circles and lines. The vision itself had a slowly moving outline that resembled somewhat a very thick letter "S" and contained brilliant blue, some white and some gold color that reminded me of sand.

The vision seemed to speak to me in some weird computer-like manner, more of a vibration than any kind of words. What bothered me was that it was outlined in black, which might have stood for outer space; I'm not sure. However, since I believe that black in a vision reflects death, illness and depression, its very presence gave me pause. I demanded it leave. However, it stayed for about ten minutes. I had to become very firm before it finally left. It was a delayed vision and transpired while I was working on this very book at my computer. I have never had an apparition so brilliant that lasted so long. The timing of this experience is also very interesting; it happened in the afternoon of November 8, 2011, when an asteroid passed between the Earth and the moon.

There is a very ancient method to travel to outer space. Lay down outside in a quiet, secure, comfortable place with your head pointing north. Say out loud your intention to project upward. Then simply relax and gaze straight up until you do. Because I'm a city dweller, I haven't tried this method, but it does sound enticing.

Astral Projection to a Physical Object

From my experience this type of projection requires caution. Meditating on places beneath you when sitting or located directly to the south of you while lying down could activate lower energies. To exit the lower etheric, you look upward and seek beautiful color. And as I've explained earlier, if you don't like your trip, out loud say "no" and move your fingers and your toes so that it will end.

You can approach this type of astral projection using two entirely different methods. The first has more details to consider but should become more vivid; the second is much more relaxed.

The First Approach: Choose an object that reflects a little light and is of a positive color. Never project to anything the color of black, brown, blood red, or grey. The color of your object will influence the type of astral projection you will have, so be careful.

Before you project you should: (1) Place your hands on both sides of the object to be visited. You will remember that feeling and it can be used later to help anchor you near the item. (2) Examine the object with your face right up next to it from many different angles. Remember how it looks. When you have your astral projection, you will be very small and real close to it. However, your vision of the item will not split into two as it does on the physical plane. (3) Look at the room from the perspective of being very close to your item, that will help you locate yourself later and the experience will be more real. (4) Place the object you want to visit so that you will not project in a straight line. If you travel in a curve to get to your destination, once you're there you won't have the feeling that you cannot move around it. (5) Kiss and stroke the object so that you can use the memory as a tool. (6) If you are astral projecting to something like a bowl or dish, I have found the memory of pinching the rim helps.

To put it very simply, if you want to astral project, you start by simply imagining yourself there; become emotionally attached to the object; and then you work at that vision until it is as real as you are now in the physical. Your imagination and emotion become your bridge.

As I've mentioned earlier, the physical body is meant to experience the physical plane. When you project, you'll be in astral energy projecting to an astral counterpart of something, sometimes very close to the physical but still in the astral. There could be some distortion.

One time, I had an projection to a vase located on my bureau which was covered by a white cloth. During the projection, the cloth extended over the bureau's edge by about an inch but on the physical plane the cloth did not meet the edge of the bureau. The astral projection was very real, vivid and beautiful. I was tiny and the vase was gigantic. I was able to move all around the vase and viewed it from a whole different perspective. I cannot put into words the wondrous feelings I had.

You will experience a different reality. Expect to be very emotional, very small, and objects very large. You can travel all around an object and go through it. To make your experience more intense, look for shading, depth, and details. Give yourself commands to make your experience more clear. Except for your projected hands, you will be very small so you can also have some fun during a projection by jumping inside an object like a bowl or vase.

Keep in mind the scale of 1-10 for astral projection. One being the energy you send when you glance at something, ten being just as real as you feel right now. Get stubborn and emotional but yet relaxed during your projection and don't settle for anything less than ten. Attitude is very important.

Use a strong emotional motivation to help you project like the word "freedom." If you like to dance, imagine yourself dancing while exploring the object; maybe kiss it. Do whatever it takes to enjoy the experience.

Keep the actual projection very simple. Pretend you are already wherever it is you want to be. If you are not at ten on the scale, keep working at it until you are, but make sure it's fun.

You might be fully centered in the astral projection energy only, or you might be centered in both your physical body and outgoing energy. Either way is great. To strengthen your projection, listen for the ringing in your ears to become louder and the pitch to become higher.

If you are projecting to an object that is placed on a table, first project a pair of hands on either side of the object to act as your anchor. Remember the sensation of touching the table. With other projected hands, touch your object; kiss it; look for shading, depth, and detail. If your breathing is noticeable, you're too tense. If you can feel any part of your physical body, that will distract you. Don't make more than one mental attempt at traveling to your object so your energies will not become fragmented. Move around it and view it from different angles. It might take more than one session to get the reality you want.

It's a common occurrence for the vision of the object to instead come to you. When that happens, you need to mentally place it back where it belongs. Project a pair of hands to the table or wherever the object is in the physical. Pay attention to the sensation of feeling.

The Second Approach: Maybe you don't want to put a lot of effort into this and just want something more simple and direct. I can relate. Here's a fairly easy way to have an astral projection to an object in a room.

If you are one who watches television late at night, get very comfortable maybe in a reclining chair, comfortable enough to doze but with your back cushioned so that it is fairly straight, and be sure to have your remote nearby. During the commercials lower the volume way down and gaze at some object in the room that reflects a little light; this will establish a bridge. Later, when the television has been turned off, when it is very quiet and the light is very dim, just gaze again at your object until you start to doze. Because the easiest part of you to project is your hands, start by imagining what it would feel like to touch it. You should easily project to it, if you can control your mind.

The object you project to can be a destination, that in itself is very exciting; or it can be a springboard to other realities. If you are determined, you will succeed. It's well worth the effort; it will change you forever.

Astral Projection Visits to the Deceased

First, remember he/she must be willing to contact you as well. If there was anger, guilt or fear coming from either side in your relationship, it might take them some time to release it, just like it is for us here on Earth. And the deceased are busy up there learning things probably beyond our comprehension. They might even be preparing to reincarnate.

There are a lot of factors to think about, one of the most important being that time is an illusion. For instance, you might contact your parents or other older relatives as they appeared and related to you when you were a child, re-experiencing the hopefully wonderful, unconditional love you received from them.

I have read, and it's part of my experience, that once older people enter the higher worlds of the astral plane, the appearance they choose to give usually changes and they start to appear as they did on Earth in their mid-thirties. A child reportedly will mature.

If your objective is to give and receive unconditional love, to say goodbye, or to make sure they are okay, that's very good. If you want material guidance from them, then you're encouraging haunting and that's not a good path for them or for you.

To visit, first meditate on a picture taken in happy times, hold something they handled frequently. The block method below is a good technique to contact them or use any method that appeals to you. It might take more than one attempt, but your efforts will be noticed. Some kind of response should be received either right away or within a day or two.

You could find your loved one in the light at the center of one of your tunnels, waiting for you in a pine grove, in a lucid dream, or simply fly into the sky and locate your loved one out there. Perhaps instead, as happened with me, your visitors will come to you at a time when they are ready.

The Block Method

This method is designed with the practical person in mind, those of us who set a goal and then take positive, well-thought-out, basic steps to achievement without wasting valuable time.

When in deep meditation, this technique will become much easier than it sounds right now.

Start by intensely (but still very relaxed) focusing on the screen formed by your closed eyelids. Pretend that it is one side of a solid, touchable block and that each side of the block looks exactly the same. Make believe that you can move slowly to view the other sides by traveling around it on the outside. When it becomes very real, forget the block and you're out. If you don't have a destination in mind, you might be right back in the physical.

The Ascension

The ascension is the ultimate projection. Therefore, I want to include teachings given to me by my spiritual guides.

Almost all of us have had uncountable lifetimes progressing through the animal kingdoms and then through the human. We are making much progress; but we have much to learn from each precious life. We study intensely during the time between incarnations to choose the best path to take next.

The word "ascension" means different things to different people. As the word is used here, it is an individual embrace of God and a very powerful acknowledgment of the light and energy of the Creator. It is not a return to God, because it is impossible to really leave. If we did, we would no longer exist.

The journey of the ascension is an automatic, individual process with no need for outside help. Everyone is always on this journey both in this lifetime and in others because that is the sole purpose for life. You see, since we are a projection of God, we will ultimately realize we are already ever and ever closer to God.

To speed the process up, you could go about your daily activities meditating on and being in the embrace of the Violet Consuming Flame of Forgiveness and Mercy which will transmute low energy to high spiritual energy. In addition, while in deep meditation, visualize a white sphere of light surrounded by a beautifully vibrating, golden yellow light. You will eventually go wherever your attention takes you. The more you follow this instruction, the faster illness and poverty will leave, the better and happier your whole life will become both here and in the lives to follow.

You do not have to leave the physical plane to make this progress, although you might. You are always in the perfect place at the perfect time. And making ever more progress to the ascension is the best thing we can do for all humanity because we are all so intimately connected.

And the individual act of the ascension never ever stops.

PART THREE, MY ADVENTURES

These trips, arranged by my guides, usually occurred immediately following a technique. Sometimes I built up energy and they just happened later, some came in a vivid dream, some as I awoke in the morning. Two happened while I was very relaxed watching television.

Grouped into two types of experiences, the first holy and wonderful, the second sometimes very difficult but things I needed to see and/or do.

I'm including these two sections so that you will know what to expect. I hope the difficult projections do not discourage you. And I hope the beautiful ones will encourage.

I feel it's only fair to be totally honest. There are no exaggerations; everything reported is as it actually happened. A lot of them I recorded about seven years ago in my journal; the rest came recently when I made the request to my guides for information for this book.

Group A, Holy and Wonderful

My tunnel became God and love. I was told to focus on becoming the love, light and energy for which I search.

%%% astral projection %%%

While praying for help, I saw a vision of Mother Mary carrying the Christ child. She handed me the baby who melted into my heart chakra. I then meditated on the light to the north of my head and saw an arm reaching for me.

%%% astral projection %%%

While going about my daily activities, I saw a white and golden light for a fraction of a second and felt the strong presence of my deceased father, a very comforting experience.

%%% astral projection %%%

I had a dream of the head of Beloved Master Jesus. It was almost like a statue in a holy church came alive.

%%% astral projection %%%

To prepare, I massaged my head and did the Yoga sun-piercing breath. While meditating on a violet crystal, I asked to see my spiritual guides. Amazing spheres of brilliant colored light appeared. I saw a pink spirit and a golden flame baby which I brought to my heart chakra. The face of a happy young man, looked Arabic, smiled at me. My tunnel rotated very fast and pointed very high.

%%% astral projection %%%

Using the block method, I stepped behind my screen and found myself in very high, scarce clouds and saw the lights of a city far below.

%%% astral projection %%%

Starting with the yoga headstand and sun piercing breath, I then meditated on a small pine tree. There were lots of vivid scenes of a forest. I was offered an astral projection to a Christmas gathering but refused it. Rays from the "Sun of Even Pressure" (a St. Germaine teaching) and visions of mountain peaks presented themselves.

%%% astral projection %%%

My deceased father led me to a time when I was about three-years old when many people surrounded me with love. My parents, aunts, and uncles were all there. It was strange to experience myself at this age and to see my older relatives so young and vibrant. I then went back even more in time briefly to my mother's womb.

%%% astral projection %%%

I had a vision of a man in a white robe with lots of brown hair and a brown beard.

%%% astral projection %%%

As I woke up one morning, I experienced an astral projection of flying over trees during a bright sunny day, a magnificent trip.

%%% astral projection %%%

While having an astral projection to either a future world or an alternate reality, I saw many tall buildings and lots of people. To get from one building to another they did not have to leave one place and walk across a street. They just got into small elevator-like rooms and were safely "sling shotted" to specifically designed areas going from building to building.

%%% astral projection %%%

One evening I meditated on a random star in the sky and attempted to send and receive energy. Later I saw the Christ child over my head descending down to my heart chakra. I remembered the star and felt flooded with tremendous energy as though there was some type of sacred communication.

%%% astral projection %%%

I was visited by a golden light breaking forth in the sky through the shadows.

%%% astral projection %%%

I experienced a full bodied, etheric projection into a hazy white world. I became my ghost.

%%% astral projection %%%

In the early morning as I woke, I saw two little shy and quiet girls in simple, homemade-looking clothing and a very vibrant little boy with dark hair and eyes. I had a strong feeling they were previous incarnations of my present three children.

%%% astral projection %%%

As I first laid down, without any preparation, the energy was just waiting for me. I could hear a very loud ringing and felt strong vibrations of electricity. Right after I closed my eyes there appeared on my screen many settlers from frontier days, American Indians dancing, and people in stage coaches. The vision stayed for quite a while.

%%% astral projection %%%

There was a small sphere of white and gold light, like a Christmas tree ornament. Several days later I again saw a small sphere but of a medium shade of blue light.

%%% astral projection %%%

While in a deep meditation, there were deep purple, gold and white spheres of small light. As I pleaded for help, golden angels enfolded me. Many arms were reaching to pull me out and upward. I was told to meditate on the blue light at my throat chakra for the power to accomplish the positive.

%%% astral projection %%%

As I awoke in the early morning, my head seemed to be elongated. While I meditated on my higher mental body, a connection came. I then meditated on my heart chakra and also felt a connection. Some kind of initiation or stronger bond seemed to take place.

%%% astral projection %%%

A golden flame appeared and I realized my mind directs where I go. I alone am in control of my ascension to the light and must focus mostly on that.

%%% astral projection %%%

I meditated for about one hour each on the heart and just above the crown chakras. Later I saw a large (about one half my size) blue and white spirit real close to me on my right side. It was an overwhelming experience which I cannot stop thinking about. Earlier that day I had seen a blue sphere that was larger than I normally see, but not as large as this.

%%% astral projection %%%

I had a vivid dream about a large stone castle apparently built into the side of a mountain. There was a protected walkway around the outside of the top, but it abruptly stopped, revealing a very long dangerous drop.

%%% astral projection %%%

A blue and white light spirit appeared just for a moment.

%%% astral projection %%%

I was in a sea of light, like a cell in the body of God, all part of each other, all one.

%%% astral projection %%%

While flying above the Earth, I felt tremendous love radiating from the trees and the Earth. It was wonderful freedom. I then flew very high above the clouds.

%%% astral projection %%%

As I laid myself down to sleep, I immediately flew over great expanses of multicolored lights.

%%% astral projection %%%

During the commercials one night while watching television, I wondered if Beloved Master Jesus would teach me. He appeared in an overpowering deep rose color.

%%% astral projection %%%

I saw a hole in the sky with an angel showing me the way to go through it. I moved closer to the opening and saw many colored lights reminding me of Christmas.

%%% astral projection %%%

During meditation, the screen before my eyes was at the crown of my head. I was looking upward through my Third Eye.

%%% astral projection %%%

I saw a border of blue around the screen my closed eyelids make.

%%% astral projection %%%

It was my deceased mother's birthday. In the physical, I saw a license plate that read: "me mere". This is French for grandmother and that is what my children and grandchildren called her. Later that day I had a wonderful meditation and saw tremendous light. I felt the presence of God more intensely than ever before.

%%% astral projection %%%

I heard my deceased mother say very clearly: "Yvette, are you all right?"

%%% astral projection %%%

Upon waking, I was playing with a small, white, brilliant light which somehow I knew was a prayer I had made the day before.

%%% astral projection %%%

For a moment, I was looking downward from the side of a very tall mountain bathed in bright daylight. There was much light-green color emanating from the pine trees.

%%% astral projection %%%

There were trees, mountains, and ocean. While stopping over a wooded area, I found a wild rabbit that is still with me.

%%% astral projection %%%

The space above my head was wonderful gold light. Inside there was a group of spirits worshiping God. I asked if I could take a gift. A male spirit answered "certainly". I scooped a small amount of light which then flowed down to my heart chakra. In this light I saw the suffering of Beloved Master Jesus, three wise men, the meditating Buddha, a tabernacle of gold with gold beads strung like pearls. Amazing!

%%% astral projection %%%

I experienced a wonderful projection to a wooded area, lots of movement.

%%% astral projection %%%

I projected to a crystal and moved all around it. I was tiny; it was gigantic. The experience was life altering.

%%% astral projection %%%

When I astral projected to a bowl of alfalfa sprouts, I found it to be boring. To make it more real, I flew from a great distance and crashed into the bowl going right through it. It seemed necessary to have fun. I then sat inside the bowl with the alfalfa sprouts and that was fun.

%%% astral projection %%%

While again attempting to project to my bowl of alfalfa sprouts, I met a guide who tried to help. He and I were looking at the bowl together. When my mind started to wander, he talked to me and brought my concentration back. I wondered if I was looking at what he really was and immediately I saw him instead as a pair of brilliant blue eyes.

%%% astral projection %%%

I meditated on my crown chakra, located at the very top of the head. I saw beautiful blue-violet light which seemed to open to a pathway of white. There were spirits extending their hands to help me enter. Once I went through there were three angels of beautiful rainbow-colored light who brought me upward to a treasure box filled with holy light.

%%% astral projection %%%

I was meditating on the light at the center of my tunnel when a spiritual guide stepped through and gave me Holy Communion. I recognized him from previous astral projection experiences. It was a holy and wonderful experience and I am very grateful.

%%% astral projection %%%

During an astral travel adventure of mine, I flew to a large brick wall. I could neither fly around nor over so I climbed it. When I got to the top, there was another "me" climbing up on the other side. When I saw her, I was too shocked to speak; but she managed to say "God bless you." I then found myself back in my physical body, but still quite startled.

%%% astral projection %%%

While meditating on my heart chakra, there was a sudden release of tension and I saw just the head of a very anguished man leave me.

%%% astral projection %%%

I was practicing astral projection to an object on a table. I chose a pine cone for this adventure. Instead of going to the table I was repeatedly drawn outside to a wooded area where pine trees grow.

%%% astral projection %%%

A friend reported that when she awoke one morning she saw another manifestation of herself quietly looking back.

%%% astral projection %%%

A relative projected to outer space where he remained still and was in awe of the beautiful lights and energy that surrounded him.

%%% astral projection %%%

After some preparation, I focused all my attention straight upward in a futile attempt to have an astral projection to outer space. After about twenty minutes of seeing no lights and experiencing no energies, I became very discouraged and pleaded for some return for all my effort. I was then blessed with two rectangular-shaped gifts of sunlight which I was able to embrace and take back down to the physical plane. They are still with me.

%%% astral projection %%%

I was meditating and chanting the AUM, when I was filled with beautiful colored shades of yellow with gold. After a while I tried to be filled with pink and then blue but I could not get the same brilliance. The message I received was to meditate more on pink for energy and love, and blue for the power to overcome and to accomplish.

%%% astral projection %%%

Sometimes I astral travel to the center of the Earth and experience overwhelming energies reminding me of a time when I was a very young child and remembered those same feelings.

%%% astral projection %%%

As I laid down, after very little preparation, I found myself flying over city landscapes. I saw women wearing long skirts, horse-drawn carriages, and some automobiles that appeared as they were in the beginning of the 20th century. I also saw the property where I grew up as it was long before I was born. The people were not ghost like; they appeared to be going about their normal daily activities. The flying was uncontrolled by me. It was a very invigorating and interesting trip which lasted maybe five minutes or so.

%%% astral projection %%%

I found myself in a dark cave-like place. I couldn't see anything except beautiful light glowing outside of the cave. I kept poking my head out to see the light and then withdrawing back into the cave. I was told that was how I am living my life. I should leave the cave and stay in the light.

Group B, the Difficult

The following experiences taught me a lot about the meaning of life. Let me warn you, they are depressing. It's why I try not to travel to other lifetimes anymore but sometimes my guides have other ideas.

I have read books that say to protect oneself in the white light when having an astral projection. I find this works for a short time. When my attention starts to focus on the trip, the energies of the trip just take over. If I was always centered in a white mantel for protection, I would not have learned what I did. I believe even though some projections our guides bring us to appear to be extremely difficult, it's meant for us to face that part of life.

I believe these are lifetimes of mine. However, we are all so closely connected who really knows for sure. Some of these experiences I flew in, others I was just there.

%%% astral projection %%%

I was in a parking lot loading groceries into the trunk of my car in physical reality. I heard a robot-sounding voice say: "This is the time we agreed upon." I instinctively knew it was talking about my death. I argued back. After all, I did have three children to help raise. I then amazingly separated into two. There was the one standing by my car and the one further back close to the sound of the voice. A speeding car filled with teenage boys suddenly appeared and ran into the "me" standing by my car. I remember feeling no pain but a lot of pressure on my chest. The surviving "me" then saw the spirit of the other floating up into the sky. I was much shaken and went immediately home and laid down. I then heard my two daughters, like in a dream, discussing the last time they saw me alive.

I often wonder what happened to the "me" who floated away.

%%% astral projection %%%

I seriously considered not including the following experience, but I believe it's only fair to be honest. I warn you, reading it might change your mind about attempting astral travel.

Having prayed for quite a while for help to stay more focused on the spiritual side, especially the ascension, early one morning my prayers were answered but in a way I will always have problems accepting. I woke up to a projection that is the most powerful and chilling I have ever had. It's taken me quite a while to recover.

I projected to a future or parallel time and very closely gazed at my own rotting corpse.

%%% astral projection %%%

I saw simple buildings surrounding a large cathedral, all in the overpowering shadow of Beloved Master Jesus carrying his cross with the crown of thorns on his head. His shadow was immense, dark, and depressing to the people.

%%% astral projection %%%

It was evening time when I flew in. I saw many dead men lying in the street. They had no hats but were all wearing winter jackets. I moved into their future, saw many houses, and traveled down their then empty streets. It's strange that there were no women nor children, neither dead nor alive.

%%% astral projection %%%

I first floated onto a scene in the middle of a wooded area where there were many different hazy colors in the trees. Evidently I was not close enough to the physical and was drawn out. I flew in again and saw that the colors were from dead bodies of women and children hanging in the trees. Horrified I left. A third time I was drawn back but to a later time. I saw a man digging a grave for a young boy who wore brown woolen knickers. I was drawn into the consciousness of this man whose horrible emotional pain was unbearable. He was thinking with much intensity that he had to dig very deep to protect the corpse from animals. I believe my presence and my energies helped him for a short time, but I'm not sure. If I was of assistance, I hope others slipped in later. I do not know.

%%% astral projection %%%

I came upon a scene by the edge of the ocean. There was a young man slowly riding a horse with a group of people who were walking. He was wearing armor on the top half of his body. A huge wave came and he was taken. Because the armor was so heavy, he could not even swim. I slipped inside. I did not experience his actual drowning, but I think my presence helped him.

I stayed at the scene only up in the sky looking down. The wave had also taken some of the people who had been walking by the shore including a young girl. I picked up on what she was thinking. It had been her responsibility to care for a baby. She knew that the baby was dead and felt terrible because she believed it was her fault. She saw me, was drawn up to me, and gazed into my eyes. She was searching for some kind of guidance, but I had no idea what she saw or what to tell her. I felt I was not the one who should have been there. All I could mentally say to her was: "it's okay."

As I was drawn out, I saw a much smaller group of people trudging away from the ocean. Their heads were down.

%%% astral projection %%%

Located on the side of a mountain, there was a huge stone castle which had many jagged edges of rock. I was part of a group of very intense people just outside. It seemed we were not worthy to enter the castle from the front. Because I was small and agile, I had been selected to deliver something of great importance to people waiting inside. I have no idea what it was. I climbed very high while hugging the castle the best I could to some kind of small opening in the rock. I was petrified.

%%% astral projection %%%

I was a toddler who lived on the side of the road in the dirt because sometimes people in carriages would throw food my way. I ate bugs as well. There was a memory of being hurt by a large wheel. During this projection, I felt no physical pain but I believe I was again run over by a large wheel and this time I died.

%%% astral projection %%%

I saw myself as two beings--one of white light who shut a heavy, large metal door leaving the second "me" inside a dark room with monsters.

%%% astral projection %%%

I was a member of a close band of men who rode very fast on horses, killed many people, and destroyed much. We used fire and had been burnt myself. Many injuries were taken for granted. My clothing and my body were very dirty. Some nights I could not sleep when it was my turn to guard part of the perimeter around the campfire while others slept.

My projection also brought me to the time just after his death. He was screaming into a void for a meaning to his life. I'm sure he saw me.

%%% astral projection %%%

From a very ancient time, I felt the emotion and heard a young man crying out for justice. He was part of a group of slaves and was severely whipped when any one of them did something wrong. Being young, healthy, and strong, he was able to survive the beatings whereas the guilty party might not. I can only imagine that guilt was being used by the owners for control.

%%% astral projection %%%

I was tiny and part of a small group of very fearful people huddled in a corner in the dark. The terror and then the memory of soft fur remain with me. Even in this lifetime, I see evil in cats.

%%% astral projection %%%

In the physical, while preparing a meal in my kitchen, I suddenly thought of an easier and better way which I immediately used. I then felt the presence of two young military men. One said: "So are you now going to tell her what to do and she will just do it?" The other replied: "It's not like I'm going to tell her to commit suicide or something."

%%% astral projection %%%

While watching television one night, during the commercials I was visualizing the sky filled with stars in preparation for an attempt to project. My guides, however, had a different plan. They did not want to wait and blessed me with the following astral projection.

There was a stone cathedral that looked very old. Before I floated inside, I viewed it from several different angles. After I entered, I saw a small group of monks standing two by two forming a short line. They were all very serious and depressed.

%%% astral projection %%%

At one time I was very determined to grow spiritually by doing two hours of deep meditation each day. One evening, after only one hour, I started to have thoughts like: "It won't hurt anything if I just skip one hour tonight." "Why am I doing this anyway?" A very large, three-headed snake then appeared directly in front of me. I saw that one of its heads was mouthing the very words I was thinking.

%%% astral projection %%%

I dreamt I was third in a long line outside a cage full of hungry lions. The first man in line was dragged by a guard into the cage. While he was screaming and being mauled, an angel appeared and handed the man in front of me a gun with one bullet. We all screamed "Kill the guard." And he did.

Our rejoicing didn't last but a few seconds when we saw the man in front of me, with his head held low, slowly walking on his own accord into the cage. An angel appeared and handed me a gun with one bullet. The man in the cage screamed at me to kill him. I knew he had walked into the cage himself so I did not feel he was worthy of my one precious bullet. The people at the back of the line screamed at me to kill a lion; but I knew that would not really help much because the cage was so full of the hungry beasts. The woman behind me quietly told me to kill myself, but that was certainly not appealing.

I really wanted to shoot my precious bullet into the screaming horde of people, because the noise and the fear were overwhelming. Instead I prayed and asked God for guidance. I was told to simply put the gun down and walk away.

I believe the message of the dream was to not become too emotionally involved in the activities of life.

%%% astral projection %%%

I was drawn inside a young man standing in a field of dirt. His filthy and disheveled appearance was of one living in dire poverty. He was trampled by another man wearing armor and riding a horse. The victim had no resentment; his belief was that he was worth nothing. The man in armor, however, was some kind of knight and believed to have every right to do whatever he chose.

%%% astral projection %%%

I tried to fly over the trees, but could not. Drawn back to my tunnel, I found very little light, instead many brown clouds, the astral counterpart of depression and my feeling of being "out of sorts."

%%% astral projection %%%

He was a military young man, heavy set, and physically and mentally very strong and powerful. Through astral projection I was drawn into his anguished but determined mind. It was a time from the distant past but for me seemed the present moment, the Colonial period in the American colonies. He was English and could only relate to the English point of view, which he considered to be an orderly and prosperous way of life. There was a young female child that he held in his mind for whom he wanted a better future. He could not understand the opposition and was wondering if he could actually kill or hurt any of them. He believed those opposed to the English were extremely confused and ignorant, but some were his family and very angry with him, including his very father.

%%% astral projection %%%

During an astral projection journey I came upon great stacks of human beings, still alive and moaning. I could see each stack had vast lifetimes and a single faint being of light who seemed to be growing with them. And I got just a glimpse of great light above. There was such immense suffering that I begged to know why. Why such agony to reach the light? I was told in my head quite simply and without emotion that we are the beings who have chosen free will. Our lives thus reflect a constant choice between the light and the agony of darkness.

%%% astral projection %%%

I had an astral projection to a previous life when I lived on a large island and was extremely powerful until one day the waves came and flushed us all out to sea. My last thoughts were not of fear but surprise that something so horrible could happen to a favored one like me.

%%% astral projection %%%

I warn you the following true story is pretty gross and shocking but also very interesting.

While slowly coming out of a deep meditation, my eyes came upon a cockroach running across the floor. I was drawn inside it for a couple of seconds. It felt a great urgency to get to the other side of the room, but at the same time it was petrified. It was very surprising to me that I could relate to its emotions. I came back with a start and very quickly got up and stepped on it.

%%% astral projection %%%

I was very small and laying on the ground. I remember this large brown boot coming at me and kicking me. There was not so much pain as pressure that lasted only a fraction of a second and I passed on.

%%% astral projection %%%

March/April 2014 Update

I have no idea of how many heaven worlds there are (maybe endless) or even what you, my readers, would consider a heaven world. From my experience, it's a place of tremendous love and beautiful, circular light where nothing from the physical plane matters. The following is how I have learned to visit them.

It helps a lot if I visualize positive colored light throughout my day and to candle-flame gaze. As with other astral projection attempts, I lay down flat on my back, hard mattress, head pointing to the north. I ask out loud for control of my mind and the experience. Next I meditate on my heart, throat, and center of my head chakras. Then my procedure changes as I take very deep breaths. On the inhale my mouth is closed. On the exhale, with my lips in a circular pattern like I'm going to whistle, I gently blow my breath upward. You can start your astral projection by paying close attention to your upward flowing breath. You'll notice that the screen your closed eyes make changes into a tunnel going upward. Center your attention in the very center of that tunnel. If you do not see a tunnel, move your closed eyes in a circular motion until you at least see a few circular lines.

You'll find beautiful colored light and a feeling that nothing matters but that light. The concept of there being an up and down makes no more sense. If you go to the left or the right you end up in the same place because you will be in a circular world. After a while I find that it doesn't matter whether I've projected or not because I find the beautiful colored light is within me as well as outside of me. It's God-given energy within all of us, otherwise we wouldn't be alive.

Each attempt will become more and more real. I have personally found such meditation brings an easing of emotional pain, improved energy, and a new, positive meaning towards life.

On a few occasions, while in such deep meditation, I have seen a head of a spirit leaving me. I have no idea if they are from past or alternate lifetimes or just wandering spirits, maybe both. Anyway I'm glad when I see one leave because I know from their appearance that they're not of the highest of light (at least mine aren't).

%%% astral projection %%%

Again, while in deep meditation, I touched upon the extraordinary vibration where only love, peace and beautiful light exist. I wanted to stay forever, but then a thought passed through of how I would word this experience and it all very sadly ended. I do so want to go back.

%%% astral projection %%%

A while ago I had prayed for a visit to one of the heaven worlds. It happened about a week later in a deep meditation when I wasn't expecting it.

I flew into a beautiful golden temple. The color gold was inside and almost everywhere, giving off the vibration of holiness. I saw an angelic looking spirit of great light shimmering with all the rainbow colors. She was so overpowering I could barely glance in her direction. She then held my hands and the journey ended.

%%% astral projection %%%

I asked for a trip to a heaven world. It came real fast, not as clear as I wanted but still very real. I flew to the same spirit I had previously encountered in the golden temple. This time it was only her that I saw, no temple. Again she was holding my hands. It was like she had never stopped holding my hands.

She had all the colors within her but this time instead of picking up on the golden light I experienced the pink predominately. Could she be my mother God?

My telephone rang (a wrong number) and the visit ended. I want to go back to her. I feel there's no place else worth going.

%%% astral projection %%%

I asked to project to a heaven world again and so I did.

There were swirling colored rays of light circling everywhere. I noticed that pink and violet were the ones I could not see as clearly as the others. Those must be the rays I must practice visualizing.

It was so beautiful I did not want to leave.

%%% astral projection %%%

I know there is a great heaven probably in the etheric where the plants seem to have their origins. I've touched upon it in my travels and it's one of my many objectives to explore this wonderland. I believe this plane is the origin for the following experience.

Early on the morning of Mothers' Day, 2013, I requested an experience that I could share with you. It came about so fast. I had just started my meditation on my heart chakra when I started to clearly see many different-colored flowers of all types. Roses did predominate. The beauty was overwhelming. The vision lasted at least ten minutes. I didn't have the feeling of traveling anywhere; the flowers came to me, a lovely gift on Mothers' Day.

%%% astral projection %%%

I was in deep meditation on the golden light above me and I believe above everybody. The vision was so clear but then it was almost gone. The message was that I can occasionally have short visions but I have to earn the gift of being more aware of our union with the Light of God through disciplined meditation.

%%% astral projection %%%

I met this beautiful male spirit of white and gold. I believe he is the energy I left behind to enter the physical realm. He seemed to complete me. He took my hand and for a moment we were flying to a brilliant white and gold sun. I couldn't stand the intensity, the brilliance, and the trip was thus ended without me meaning to end it. I am very disappointed with myself. He stayed with me for the rest of the day. Right now it's the next day and I can tell his presence is starting to fade. But when I meditate on white and gold (my favorite colors) he reappears as strong as ever.

%%% astral projection %%%

I'm now wondering if the golden halo we all have around our heads is an extension of the white and gold chakra in the center or our heads. Maybe we all have this chakra colored the same way like the throat chakra is considered by most to be colored blue.

%%% astral projection %%%

I saw my pathway, beautiful white light, which pointed straight upward. There was a beautiful spirit of white and gold light showing it to me. The spirit called me "Judith," which even though it's not my present name, at the time seemed only correct. I glanced downward and saw the same connected pathway not bright and straight but darker and curved. I saw a gun.

%%% astral projection %%%

I now realize why I am so blessed with the presence of the beautiful gold and white spirit. I had been sick and was fed up with it. So I prayed frequently, fervently but not specifically for help from God by pleading: "Dear God, help me. Help me. Help me." And so I received His/Her help (certainly not the kind of help I had expected, but worth so much more). I'm still sick but wouldn't trade my heaven experiences for the world.

%%% astral projection %%%

The words "I Am That I Am" as you all probably know is an English translation of one of Hebrew's ancient and sacred names for God. In the English language (the only one I am familiar with) we never use the verb "am" except after the pronoun "I". Perhaps we're all named after our Creator.

%%% astral projection %%%

The following is very surreal. I very much need to write it down and share it.

I haven't projected in a while. It's springtime and I've been suffering with allergies, had some very distracting symptoms. My golden and white flame guide is still with me. I pick up on his energy whenever I try to meditate.

Today I figured it's a real good time to put allergies aside and learn more about reality. I started my meditation with an attempt to fly through nature. Instead it was a flight through golden light with my guide holding my hand. We were very tiny, about the size of two pin heads. We went to a place where time and space don't exist. I saw my many, many lifetimes all rolled into a large sphere of energy. There was love but hatred; peace but conflict; all the emotions of my many lifetimes were inside this huge ball which we circled. I wanted to know the meaning of it all. I then found myself and my guide looking at an old man dozing on a porch in a rocking chair. I then knew that my many lives were like his many dreams. I asked my guide who he was and was told that he represents me.

I'm now realizing that my life when I was much younger now feels like a dream and that my present time will someday also be dreamlike. The very present moment is all that is true. To leave the dream state I must focus on what is real--my connection to my eternal God of endless love, power and wisdom.

%%% astral projection %%%

I asked for an experience I could share with you.

Instead of projecting outward, as is my habit, I stayed inside at my heart chakra, colored rose/pink. Instead of just thinking of its location, I projected there and enjoyed the love of my Mother God more intensely. At my throat chakra I lingered longer than usual and enjoyed the power and love of my Father God. It was a strange sensation that I've had before to be looking outward while centered there. I then enjoyed the golden light of wisdom and holiness in my head.

This experience made me realize more intensely that we are all creations and a part of God. We need to look no further than inside ourselves.

%%% astral projection %%%

This is a difficult astral projection to explain.

I requested an experience I could share and benefit. I meditated on my heart, throat and center of my head chakras.

It began as a visit with many of my relatives on the other side, located on the lawn behind a house where we had many gatherings long ago. (I've experienced an astral visit to them once before.) It was so wonderful to see my aunts and uncles again as they were when I was very young. There was one exception, an elderly uncle who was sitting a little apart from the others and who looked exactly like he did the last time I saw him in the physical.

Then the vibrations changed and it turned into a visit with my parents who were also young and vibrant. It's amazing to realize that is what they have now returned to only more intensely. It was wonderful to see them so happy. I must have been experiencing their essence and they mine. It was a surreal trip like I have never had before. We were sort of gliding in huge circles. It was their faces I saw and even experienced; they faded in and out. They were not in their physical shapes but yet I knew them and could see them. There were no words or thoughts shared just tremendous joy and love.

May 2014 Update

I candle-flame gazed for about twenty minutes. I had tended to my potted plants a short time before so it was real easy to have an astral projection to them as I closed my eyes and meditated once again. From there I was taken to one of my very favorite places where lots of plants grow. I saw many flowers and young plants. It was very beautiful and energizing, very difficult to put into words.

%%% astral projection %%%

I've been thinking that if a guide is kind enough to teach astral projection to us, maybe a guide would also teach spiritual advancement, also called the ascension. I asked and the following is a response.

I was shown a very good man who lived sometime around a hundred to two hundred years ago. When I saw him he was admiring a horse and buggy that was moving down the street in front of him. He had built a major portion of the buggy, something to do with the wheels and something with the carving and the finishing of the wood. Someone else had purchased it. He had reason to be proud; it was beautiful.

I was told that his attachment to his work would be the major force that would bring him back to the Earth plane for another incarnation.

It's very easy to project to a pot of healthy plants. You'll see how you can become one with the plants and realize you are one with All That Is.

To start, carry the memory of the plants with you throughout your day. It's amazing how that memory can stay with you. As soon as you start your meditation, you'll see them in your head. To project to the pot remember what the feeling of the moist dirt is; put your hands around the edge of the pot. Feel the happiness and you're there.

Having reached the chakra in the center of my head during my meditation I was presented with different slots to pass through to experience different lifetimes. One seemed to beckon to me so I chose it.

It brought me immediately to a lifetime where I was a baby monkey or ape, something in that line of animals. I felt very small in comparison to the other animals around me. There was great love and acceptance for me simply because I existed. I remember being petted and nursed and a feeling of great happiness. I felt and saw lots of soft brown fur. There were huge trees all around us, giving a sense of security. I heard the sounds of the forest. Towards the end of the experience I did separate somewhat from the baby and I saw and felt a little of the surrounding landscape.

The journey was unbelievable.

%%% astral projection %%%

My goal was to simply visit a rock I had placed on a table in my room. Instead I felt the rock as part of God's holy creation. I lived in the present moment with it. It was Nature. I experienced the larger rock formation and part of the mountain where it originated. I felt life but not as we normally know it; it was basic, steady, awesome awareness of God.

%%% astral projection %%%

During this astral projection I was lying in a field. There was a strong man holding me down. He had some protective light armor on him; I had none. His left arm was on my throat choking me; I saw his sword coming down. There was no fear, just total numbness. I woke up startled and energized.

%%% astral projection %%%

I meditated on my heart and then my throat chakras but with a lot of distracting thoughts. I didn't expect a trip, but one came anyway as my attention reached the center of my head.

At first it was like watching television on a medium-sized screen. I kept trying to pass through the screen in an attempt to get closer, but it didn't work. I tried to feel the objects I was seeing but had no success. I had no control and found that very frustrating.

It then felt like I was in a vehicle, looking out the window, and flying over the land, but I knew from past experience that I was really stationary and the Earth (or who knows what planet) was rotating on its axis. It was just the sensation of motion.

I was over a desert where the Earth was colored red. I don't know if this was because of the angle of the sunshine or if there was an actual red color. There were lots of large dark-colored rocks. After a while, instead of rocks there were scattered trees. Then I saw water and normal-colored dirt, greens and trees, as well as some people and buildings.

It turned out to be a great trip and lasted at least fifteen minutes.

%%% astral projection %%%

I have a hard time understanding why we release wolves into the wilderness; they eat small animals. Then one day I had a very short astral projection. I saw a wolf standing still and staring right into my eyes. I felt a strong connection with it. I believe I probably was that wolf at one time.

%%% astral projection %%%

I prayed again for an experience that would teach something about control of an astral projection.

I was barely centered at my heart chakra when it started. I was flying past houses and trees at a great speed. I tried to maneuver by brushing against the trees but the uncontrollable speed was too fast and the scene kept changing constantly. After probably a half hour I was inspired to think of the color blue and my physical throat. Immediately my projection changed. I was then very tiny and located in a field, much more to my liking. There was little motion and only when I directed it. Things weren't as clear anymore. It was more in the etheric plane. I believe I experienced the essence of the plants. I felt the joy of Nature.

It seems like a good method that I will attempt again when I feel out of control.

%%% astral projection %%%

To make my experience as real as possible I projected four legs and was walking down a country road like a dog would using the sensation of touching the road as a tool. I enjoyed seeing the very large trees and the different houses.

%%% astral projection %%%

I woke up real early, around 4 a.m., a good time for astral projection. I started to meditate on my heart chakra. Not because of any choice of mine I found myself flying over a busy town during the time of the Old Western Frontier. It was extremely fast and uncontrolled, nowhere near the realism I prefer. I thought of my throat and the color blue. Immediately the scene stopped and I was in a barroom of long ago; there were guns everywhere. My immediate goal was to make the experience more intense. I touched the floor which really helped me to locate myself in the room. There was a banister that led up a stairway and so I grabbed onto it. It was strange because at that point there was only the floor and the banister that were very real to me. My experience then stopped. I guess the lesson was over.

%%% astral projection %%%

It's my habit to visualize whatever my astral projection goal is throughout my day. I was watching the news and a boring part came up so I used that time and practiced visualizing the object I was working on at the time. I looked upward. Suddenly I felt like I was inside a beautiful cathedral with stained glass windows. It was circular. I looked at the top and there was an opening filled with white light. It lasted only a few moments, but was life altering.

I can project to an object in a room, but I sure had help with what has just transpired. The timing is a mystery, but that's happened to me before. I'm relaxed while watching television and I do get bored with it a lot.

From that experience I have learned that my personal goals are not the most important things in my life. What's important is to focus on the spiritual side.

%%% astral projection %%%

I projected to a small folding table and saw my parents as they were during their retirement years. I realized then that the card table I was projecting to was the very same one they had used to play cards which they loved to do.

%%% astral projection %%%

I woke with the message that the reason I see a dish I am attempting to project to at a distance is because that is how I am gazing at it while I prepare. I now position myself so that my head is right next to it and my nose touches it. I carry this vision in my head throughout my day.

%%% astral projection %%%

I found myself flying over and through treetops. I did remember that I could change my direction and/or touch the trees for more clarity. I knew I could fly to the clouds and float down to another reality. However, the experience was too spectacular; I just relaxed and relished the trip. It was awesome.

%%% astral projection %%%

I was trying to project to a pitcher located on a table nearby; instead I flew through the woods. I did stop a couple of times to visit with some beautiful wild flowers. It was a wonderful trip.

%%% astral projection %%%

It's so very important to write these experiences down no matter how awesome they may be. Because they are not from the physical plane, they fade from memory so easily.

%%% astral projection %%%

I had prayed for an experience that I could both benefit and share with you. It started and stayed in the waking state of astral projection. I asked to meet those who are other manifestations of myself in past, future or alternate realities. It was also my very strong desire to travel upward to the light that connects us all to the God Flame.

It started as a rapid journey across the Earth and felt like when I travel through the woods only this time I traveled through a white light. One of the problems was that even though this light wasn't grey it certainly should have more brilliance and there were many holes. The message I got was that if it was as bright as I know it should be and without any holes, I wouldn't have to be here on the Earth plane. My belief of the meaning of white is twofold. First it contains the three basic colors of pink, gold, and blue, so it's ALL THAT IS. It also reflects the power of the purity of good intentions, which must be what I need to work on. I understood that part of the message almost immediately.

I traveled fast but seemed to be getting nowhere. Then there appeared medium-sized spheres of different-colored beautiful light now and then. I knew the direction I was going should be instead straight upward. I did change it but only with great effort. Many more spheres of light appeared to flash in and out. For five or ten minutes I did travel upward but not with the feeling of arriving anyplace just being.

I then saw a young man wearing a beautiful golden shirt. He was sitting in the midst of all this light. He saw me; there was no embrace or thrill of meeting. We just nodded as though we each acknowledged the other's presence. I kept on my journey. I hated to see it end.

I now realize I must meditate on the white light and visualize it as being more brilliant and focus more on the true meaning of my intentions as I continue this journey through life.

%%% astral projection %%%

I entered the doorway of an old stone building. My experience ended. There must be some reason. Hopefully, I can explore the building at another time.

%%% astral projection %%%

This morning I had a real difficult time centering myself in my meditation. I didn't expect any results. At the end I pleaded with God for more mental control. I was shown vast light directly above my head. It had all the colors of the rainbow. I was told that we all have this connection to the Godhead we just need to remember it.

July 2014 Update

I've done a lot of very exciting astral projections to many different times and dimensions and I've concluded that the best way to spend my time is to project to a Heaven world. It brings on a peaceful feeling of love for all, some physical energy, and a sense of wellbeing. I've also noticed that as I bring this energy back with me the problems in my physical world evolve into solutions. Because each human being has free will, we all have the ability to project to these sacred planes.

Let me take you one simple step at a time to visit any one of the Heaven worlds, whatever your belief and/or desired destination within these worlds may be. You first become a part of the Heaven world with all its powerful energy and sacred light and thus you are there.

Accept and then frequently meditate on physical reality as being not so much what it appears to be but something we have all contributed to the making ourselves. Each one of us is, therefore, the one in control. We may thus leave our creation whenever we choose.

My definition of "Heaven" is a holy place located beyond the physical plane. From my experience there are many such defined worlds just waiting for us to explore. I have found that space and time are part of the physical experience and thus illusions we have created to experience physical life in a methodical manner. Most Heaven worlds are way beyond space and time. They are infinite expressions of love and peace, a part of God, and God is found everywhere.

On one of the very highest sacred planes you can locate the holy energy you left behind in order to experience the physical plane and to learn whatever lessons you have come to learn. This left-behind energy is called by some the Mighty I AM Presence. To return fully and embrace the very highest of this energy is called the Ascension. Keep in mind that it's not so difficult to return to a place where part of you is waiting and that goes for all the different and majestic manifestations of Heaven. We're part of God; God is everywhere; therefore, we are everywhere. The problem is our own fear of the unknown and when viewed from the physical perspective the complete Ascension (leaving the physical permanently) has an aspect of suicide to it.

Because we're all so intimately connected in the physical world through our breath and vibrations, experiencing the Heaven worlds helps to bring the sacredness of Heaven to Earth to contribute to peace and happiness for all.

Focus for several days on what you expect and want your reality of Heaven to be and use some simple astral projection techniques that I will describe; it's that simple. Perhaps your idea is to visit the deceased, the origins of the plant worlds, or fly into sacred, brilliant, holy light; the list goes on and on. There are many places. Start by praying out loud for assistance from your high spiritual guides. At least on some of your journeys, open up and let them take you to wherever they think best. You'll be amazed.

Let me give an example of what focus does. (I warn you what you are about to read is somewhat gross.) I had just spent a lot of time and attention on a section of a short fantasy story I was writing (it never worked out). It tells the tale of a little girl trapped in the mouth of a monster and then spit out with all the force of a hurricane. The day after I finished that part of the story, I decided to go on a raw, beet juice cleanse. I eat beets all the time with never a problem. I tried my own version where I chopped up a small, raw, organic beet and blended it with a little water. I slowly drank this mixture first thing in the morning. About a half hour later I threw it all up with such a strong wind-like force I've never experienced before. I thus lived through what my focus was on for a few days and within the confines of the world I have created for myself. You can use this power to accomplish anything including projection to a Heaven world.

If you center your attention at the center of your head, you will start to see a small white light surrounded by gold appear on the screen your closed eyes make. The more you practice, the more intense your visions become and the easier it will be to enter this light.

See the energy and light as it starts to form. When you find your screen moving either inward or outward you will notice it is at your command, whichever way you choose. When outward your projections will first appear as visions that you may enter by remembering what things feel like. Of course, in the Heaven worlds there isn't much to feel like in other projections, so that could become a problem. One of the first things I sometimes find is the waiting hands of a high spiritual being so I can remember what hands feel like. However, if you bring the screen inward instead, you will find yourself in the midst of wherever it is you want to be. It's a lot easier.

Visualizing the color gold helps a lot. It brings a feeling of great holiness, very necessary to visit a Heaven world.

Don't ever get discouraged. Like any other venture, your ability might come and go like mine does. It all depends on your focus both during your meditations and throughout your daily life. When I am thinking more about the words I will write down than the sacred, holy light I long for, my ability to project wanes.

%%% astral projection %%%

For several days in my prayers I had asked over and over for trips to the Heaven worlds. This one came when I was relaxed but didn't expect it, and not with any of my usual preparations.

In my projection it was winter and snowing; I flew, while centered inside my tunnel, very fast through the woods. I was flying into a very bright light; the intensity was similar to the reflection of the sun on a piece of metal or mirror, overwhelming white sparkling with the colors of the rainbow.

The experience didn't even last a minute; maybe that short time was all the intensity I could stand. It was awesome.

%%% astral projection %%%

This time I went through my whole preparation routine. In time I did see a large sun-like sphere; but I was looking through a lot of small, dark grey, cloud-like matter. I believe I saw the astral counterpart of my many distracting thoughts.

I need to center more on the spiritual side. The only way I can do that is to pray for help.

%%% astral projection %%%

I meditated quite a while with very little results. My mind just kept wandering. I then saw a few lines of a very light tunnel with a very soft sphere of light at the center. It was nowhere near the intensity I know I can experience. Even so, I asked for and did receive a Holy Communion of Light to take with me throughout my day. That's what's really important, receiving the Light.

%%% astral projection %%%

I've been praying to visit a Heaven world. It came to me; I didn't travel to it. I felt like I was moving very fast up in the mountains, but I know I was stationary in the sky and the Earth was rotating on its axis. It just felt like fast movement. I love to gaze at the mountains and feel their holiness, so for me this was a trip to a Heaven world. At times I saw the edge of a tunnel which turned into grass and trees.

%%% astral projection %%%

I was very relaxed while lying in bed, all curled up so my focus wasn't good and the experience didn't last but a moment. I saw the faint outlines of a tunnel, no golden circular strands, but just some movement. I focused in the center and outward. Just for a fraction of a second I saw a white light; it was alive, happy, loving, and noticed me. I became filled with energy and so it ended.

%%% astral projection %%%

I saw many circular lines of beautiful color mostly golden. I could faintly see high spiritual beings of great light.

%%% astral projection %%%

I focused very intently in the center of the screen my closed eyes make. Eventually I saw the white sphere surrounded with the gold. It faded in and out at first, but then got larger and very intense. Then I saw many bright lights surrounding the gold. It became an awesome showing of the Light of God. The vision lasted about a half hour. I didn't want it to ever stop.

%%% astral projection %%%

First I meditated intently on my heart, throat, and center of my head chakras. It wasn't so much that I went someplace but became someplace. There was intense light just above my head that I knew was separated but still a part of me. There were beautifully lighted spheres of high energy life all around. I can understand where the concept of angels originated. I became so full of energy that my projection unfortunately ended. It must have lasted for at least a half hour.

%%% astral projection %%%

This morning I didn't have the feeling of going anyplace but of just becoming the Light of God more intensely. It was wonderful.

%%% astral projection %%%

In my very lucid dream I entered the sacred Light of white surrounded by gold. It felt like I was moving very fast but getting nowhere at all. Then I realized that sense of movement came from me. It was what I expected and not what was really there. I then quieted down and experienced great, overwhelming love for all. I saw a door and opened it. There was a small, black dog, the same dog that my family had owned when I was a very young child. I remembered the great love I had for that dog.

%%% astral projection %%%

We can all receive instruction through lucid dreaming; we just need to first ask before going to sleep.

In my very coherent dream I found myself in a long tunnel deep inside the Earth. The walls were of large stone which I could feel so I knew I was close to physical reality. While traveling very fast through this tunnel I kept seeing flashes of tremendous light always just around the corner. No matter how fast I ran the light was always just around the corner. I know the message is to stop running and just be this holy, awesome light.

%%% astral projection %%%

When I first went to sleep for the evening I asked for a lucid dream. I remember very clearly only that I had a great one and I would add it to this update in the morning. Morning came but I had already forgotten. Don't you make that mistake even very lucid dreams fade away so fast. Have a pencil and paper by your bed and force yourself to get right up and write something down to remember.

%%% astral projection %%%

I prayed for a visit to a Heaven world. I started my normal procedure but got no further than my heart chakra. I found it easy to center my attention there when I saw a part of the screen my closed eyes make extending downward to the center of my chest. It was my soft exhale that moved the screen downward. I then realized more fully that is a very easy way to project, maybe the only way. In order to see the color pink there, as is my habit, I visualized roses. I saw the pink in streams of holy light as well as some gold and blue. This is where our love is centered, where are energy starts.

%%% astral projection %%%

I am learning that the more I turn my physical world into a Heaven-like existence, the more visits from Heaven I receive.

August 2014 Update

In my very lucid dream, I was a sphere of white light. There were two men in human form with me. We communicated easily because all of my thoughts were visible to them. I was shown that my thoughts are an important and very open part of myself.

%%% astral projection %%%

Just before bedtime I watched a Nature program on tv. Afterwards I curled up in bed and did none of the things I tell you to do to have a lucid dream. I was tired and just wanted to have some precious sleep. Sleep didn't happen. Nature came to me for at least 45 minutes. I saw all sorts of beautiful plants. I was inspired to bring them inside of me to benefit from their holy energy. It worked. I became energized. No more sleep for me!!! The experience changed me. I now feel more in tune with Nature.

%%% astral projection %%%

I evidently received a lesson in lucid dream control. I dreamt I was in a supermarket in the produce department. For me that's the best part of the store because I'm a vegetarian. It was brimming over with all sorts of beautifully colored produce. Because I mentally prepared myself to gain control over my dreams before my sleep, I remembered to hold onto something. I grabbed a cart and started loading it up with produce, then a second cart. The dream became very real, but it ended before I could leave the store.

%%% astral projection %%%

I woke up with the reminder that on the astral plane, just like on the physical, we travel to and experience whatever and wherever our focus takes us, which is probably why I can project within Nature so easily.

%%% astral projection %%%

When I was writing this paper, I needed guidance. One evening I focused on my throat chakra colored blue and asked my question. Because of the deep breathing I did and the fact that I was tired, I fell asleep fast.

In my very vivid dream I was in a snowmobile gliding down the gentle slope of a beautiful mountain. The weather was perfect and I was having fun. Suddenly everything was in a shadow and depression smothered me. The snowmobile stopped and I got out. I didn't have any shoes and the road looked rough; a feeling of coldness came over me. I was determined to just take one step at a time and get through it. Then on a trail close to mine another snowmobile was flying by filled with happy people. Their pathway was bright and easy. I saw what I needed and got back into my vehicle. I steered in this slightly new direction and put a smile back on my face. It worked. The sun was out again and I was gliding down the beautiful slope.

I knew the answer to my question was to approach my work from a slightly different angle and enjoy the journey.

%%% astral projection %%%

I asked for a lesson and went to sleep meditating on the blue light in the center of my throat chakra.

In my very intense dream I found myself in a busy laundromat with my wet clothes in hand standing next to a dryer that was almost finished. It then stopped and a man promptly came up and emptied it. Of course he had seen me waiting. Instead of stepping aside, he put more wet clothing inside the machine. I was upset that he had not told me earlier he had additional drying to do so that I could have found another dryer or taken my wet clothes home to dry them another way.

He smiled at me, reached over for my wet clothes and put them in the dryer along with his. He simply said, "We can cooperate." I believe this is a message from a high spiritual guide, probably the same one who appeared to me a while ago as an ancient Egyptian.

%%% astral projection %%%

Having first asked for help with a health problem just before my evening sleep, I woke up with the answer that everybody has hands that heal. We just need to recognize that fact. Therefore, we can all heal ourselves. I was also reminded to live in the light of God. I am trying to focus on beautiful light throughout my day. It's easy to forget and let the boring mundane aspects of life take over.

%%% astral projection %%%

As I was entering my dream state, I requested guidance concerning my writing projects. A spectacular lucid dream then followed.

I was walking down a street accompanied by a lot of family and friends. We were going to my brother's house for dinner. I was young and wearing a very beautiful dress. About half way I stopped and changed into another beautiful dress. I was behind the others but somehow arrived at our destination ahead of them.

My sister in law and brother were preparing a large feast. I helped in the preparation. The dream ended.

In this dream the message was that even though I am making some changes to my writing, it will still be very beneficial.

%%% astral projection %%%

I had a very intense lucid dream like never before. I met a new friend. There were benches like in a large church. As I entered I noticed that she was the only one sitting alone, so I sat down next to her. I recognized her because she was a very important person, one in charge; but it was obvious that she did not recognize me. I was only a worker in this dream. However, we were both on some kind of break so that seemed to even the "playing field." We talked quite a while like any new friends would by exchanging information about our lives. At the end of the dream, she said that it was very nice to have met me. I feel that we will continue to be friends.

%%% astral projection %%%

Before I entered my sleep for the night I asked for a lucid dream that I could share. I sure got it.

I saw a much loved uncle open the backdoor to a building where I lived and was glad he still had a key. He knocked on the door to my apartment and I was very happy as I let him inside. There were some objects of mine lying on the chair where he was to sit. I reached and got most of them out of the way but a very old picture of Mother Mary remained. I was afraid he would damage it but somehow it had moved over for him. There had been problems in our family and I believe that was what the picture represented.

There were also papers that contained equations that were scattered throughout the apartment. I was ashamed to see them just lying about. I know they represented my many problems with putting my thoughts in some kind of order for this book and they also represented putting the various aspects of my life in order.

He assured me that I was making progress. He could view things from a different perspective and had a key that worked to help solve things. He put his key inside a box and turned it. My dream ended.

%%% astral projection %%%

Slowly day after day the concerns of my physical world have again taken my life over. Even my daily meditations have stopped. I still presumed my lucid dreams would continue, but they have not. I have asked my question every evening for guidance, but no answers. I have learned that lucid dreaming follows daily meditation.

As I woke this morning, I saw a vision of an elderly gentleman who told me directly that I need to meditate daily. I know my life should become a meditation.

%%% astral projection %%%

As I was relaxing to take a nap, I entered a lucid dream state, I asked for a solution to a health problem. I was shown some beautiful flowers in the daisy family. As I woke I mentally heard the word echinacea and then realized the flowers were echinacea, widely used for healing.

%%% astral projection %%%

As I went to sleep I focused inside my throat chakra, colored blue. My attention was so intense that I could see the screen my closed eyelids make as being in front of my throat. Evidently I projected to my throat.

As is my habit, I pretended to clap my hands and dance so that I could have some control over my lucid dreams. I saw either a very primitive human or animal from the ape species also clapping and dancing. I then saw a spirit rise from this being and ascend to heaven while the human or animal continued its dance.

The message I received from this experience is that sometimes spirits will attach themselves temporarily to learn. When the lesson is over, they leave.

%%% astral projection %%%

I meditated on my heart, throat and middle of my head chakras each for a short time; my intention was to experience the light more intensely. I focused upward, and then my vision came, crystal clear. Again I saw many flowers, but this was very unique. The stems and leaves appeared to be soft reminding me of velvet. The huge amount of different flowers appeared glowing with intense light intermingled with spheres of brilliant lights. It lasted a good 15 minutes. I wish I could live with that vision forever.

%%% astral projection %%%

A very, very long time ago I read a book on dream interpretation and I don't remember the name of the book or the author to give credit. It reported that food represents money and that one piece of guidance has stayed in my memory ever since. I'm no expert on traditional dream interpretation. I believe instead if you ask for understandable guidance on any subject that's what you get in your dreams and that has worked for me for many years. However, I do accept that food represents money for me anyway. I have also found that sometimes lucid dreams give clues to our future, especially the very near future.

Last night in my lucid dream there was a large taco filled with delicious food. It had been cut into three sections; the middle being much larger than the other two pieces. The middle piece was then suddenly taken away. This morning I found out that a share of money that I believe was due was legally not given to me.

%%% astral projection %%%

I went for my walk not so much deeply in Nature as just down the street; but I did study some snow-laden trees as I walked by. Shortly after I returned home I laid myself down on my back (hard mattress, back straight, no pillow, and head pointing north) and briefly meditated on my heart chakra. Almost immediately the journey started.

It started out in the woods where it was snowing with everything glistening in a white coat. I had to work on the reality a bit. It started, as they sometimes do, like a 3-D movie I was watching real close. I remembered how the feeling of touching the trees as I passed would be. It worked as it brought me pretty much into my astral projection projection.

After a while my journey slowed down a bit and there were beautiful houses, people shoveling snow, and automobiles driving slowly with their lights on.

Then there appeared large spheres of different colored light, mostly violet. Usually when this happens, all I see are the spheres. However, this time the light just blended into the background with the snow, very beautiful.

I tried to look upward, but could not. I eventually had to end this journey to start a new adventure going upward. There was what I believe an angel, even what appeared to be wings, but they faded in and out. (Who really can define what an angel is or even looks like?) I then became so energized that my journey ended.

It was a voyage to remember and treasure.

%%% astral projection %%%

I've come to suspect that we humans are a bit like a young teenage boy from many years ago who ran away from a wealthy and loving family to join the circus. After a while he realized what a better life he had at home, but the circus had moved so many times that he no longer knew how to return. He was lost.

Eventually he matured and knew enough to ask for directions which he did and they were given. It then became his choice to stay or return home.

%%% astral projection %%%

Last night I prepared simply by mentally deep breathing in the Light of God located above my head. This morning I remember a short lucid dream where I met another manifestation of myself. She was all golden light. She said: "It is finally nice to meet you." I am very grateful for my apparent relationship with her.

%%% astral projection %%%

I feel I should be open and honest with you concerning this practice. I'm no saint so sometimes I see negativity on the astral plane. This experience I am about to share is very gross. Think twice before you read further. It could give you nightmares.

Yesterday I ate a lot of sugar so I didn't sleep very well. I woke up in the middle of the night thinking that it would be an excellent time for astral projection, but it was very difficult; there were way too many foolish thoughts running through my head; and I was very restless. I begged God for help. I requested an experience I could include in this writing and also benefit. As the old saying goes, "Be careful of what you ask for."

I had a clear vision of the head of a very large, ugly, grey/brown snake very close to my head. Thankfully, it lasted not even a second. I knew from previous astral projections that sometimes this is how negative thought forms appear on the astral plane. I had been giving in to negativity which this snake feeds on and it in turn was supplying me with stupid fantasies. Even though I have seen something similar a while ago, I guess I needed a new experience to scare me straight again. I have touched upon what a segment of reality truly is and so I benefited. There is nothing that can bring a person closer to the light than not to see the light but something very negative instead. This astral snake is part of me and I must focus more on my spiritual side to dissolve it.

Astral projection will always take you to wherever your focus happens to be.

%%% astral projection %%%

The following is very difficult to put into words, but I'll do the very best I can.

This morning I have had the most profound experience of my life. It has taught me what our life force is, energy extending from brilliant, colored light.

In deep meditation sometimes we can see globes of beautiful light on the screen our closed eyelids make. I have now learned these spheres are the energy of God that keeps us alive.

For years I have found the path to projection outward to be centered right before our closed eyes. I now have been shown this screen is also the path inward. It is a spiritual blanket of energy that can be drawn inside as well by means of our breath to encounter our life force -- the power that keeps our hearts beating, our cells alive and thriving, the ability to move about.

It wasn't an experience from the astral plane but a high spiritual encounter with my true self. I am most grateful and what a joy to be able to share it with you.

%%% astral projection %%%

Again I took myself inward. It's easy. While in deep meditation focus inside your head and at the same time pay close attention to the screen your closed eyes make. The screen moves wherever you choose.

It's hard to put the following into words. I saw my whole life right there inside the screen inside my head. I felt my energy as powerful and felt lots of love. I thought of the past and I saw and remembered people, things, and events. I wondered if I could see my future and immediately I saw a horrible event in a possible future. Like before with the vision of that ugly snake, I am now scared straight once again. I will no longer travel on the pathway leading to that future. I want something a lot better for myself.

%%% astral projection %%%

We all remember events from our lives that we wish we could change for the better but believe we cannot. The following experience helps put me more at ease.

I laid straight on my back with my head pointing northward. For five or ten minutes I breathed deeply through my nose while mentally visualizing beautiful colored light entering my physical body on the inhale and extending outward to all life on the exhale.

I then saw myself as I was when very young, maybe three-years old or so. I was able to project inside my young self.

I now believe we can strengthen and heal the person we once were. You see life is not at all what it appears to be.

%%% astral projection %%%

For me and probably for you the amount of time and the intensity of spiritual meditation has a profound effect on my ability leading to astral projection. The physical location while meditating can also be of great assistance because there is a package of high energy that stays behind. If you meditate in the same places, you will pick up on it and it gets easier, deeper and more joyful.

%%% astral projection %%%

I've explained the Trinity of Sacred Colors before, but now I'm being led to an even deeper understanding.

What works for me when I'm tired is I visualize my breath as having the color of rose/pink. On the inhale I place it inside my heart chakra (center of the chest) and then with my exhale I see the Love of God extending to all mankind. Immediately I have energy.

The color blue can be used in a similar manner only centered in the throat chakra. Blue brings the Power of God to overcome the negative and to create the positive. When I meditate in this manner, immediately it helps me on my pathway.

The color of gold extending to all beings by the use of our breath brings the Wisdom of God from the center of our heads to all people everywhere forever. I have found it brings solutions to problems.

Then, of course, the three colors together, the Holy Trinity, make up the white light which brings the power of innocence to all.

Because we're all so intimately connected on higher planes and on the physical by the atoms in the air we all breathe, I believe each one of us is responsible for any negativity and for anything positive found anywhere. If we all meditate on the Light of God frequently, what a beautiful world the Earth could be.

When you get to be my age, you realize that we all have our own unique problems. Through meditation on the Light they can be conquered not only for us but for everyone.

%%% astral projection %%%

To astral project you need to control your mind. With me, for control of my wandering mind, it takes intense prayer (actually more like pleading with God).

%%% astral projection %%%

When I was younger I enjoyed skiing. Last night before sleep took over I astral projected to a snow-covered mountain and traveled real fast up and down for about ten minutes. It was a whole lot like skiing only better. What helped a lot was remembering what the feeling of holding onto my ski poles felt like.

I did have a minor problem involving seeing myself skiing. Earlier I explained that sometimes we project more than one astral body at a time, the one having the adventure and the one watching. Once I remembered this, I relaxed and more fully entered the astral body having all the fun.

%%% astral projection %%%

More and more I am realizing that solutions to problems and better ways of doing things come so much easier with meditation on brilliant golden light.

%%% astral projection %%%

I've been thinking a lot lately about how nice it would be to own a house. My astral projection, therefore, was centered on touring houses. They presented themselves one right after another, all different and all so fast. Sometimes I saw people and wondered if any of them could see me. I suppose I would appear as a ghost to them. I need to turn my focus inward to the spiritual. My true goal is to explore the Heaven worlds during an astral projection and to receive guidance.

%%% astral projection %%%

After my meditation I had a hard time seeing my tunnel; so I tried over and over by circling my closed eyes. Finally a few lines appeared on the screen my closed eyes made. I focused in the point I figured was the center and looked for movement. There appeared two men sitting on horses in full armor. My only thought was that it must have been very uncomfortable for them.

%%% astral projection %%%

This morning I had many rambling thoughts and didn't get any further than my heart chakra, but I did have some moments of extending love to all. Then there came a visit of unconditional love from a mother figure from either the ape or the monkey species. I have no idea of her size. I've reported on visiting her before, but that time it was to her whole family and in her setting. This time it was much more personal with such intense love extending from her to me across time and across species. I can't put into words how grateful I am to her.

%%% astral projection %%%

As I went to sleep I asked out loud for a lucid dream I could both share with you and learn. I asked how to make spiritual progress. I dreamt I was traveling in a car but did not know where I was going. There were two others traveling with me, a female and a male. They both needed to be dropped off at their separate homes. The female knew where she was going and gave me directions. The male knew how to get from her place to his. As I awoke, I knew that she represented the female aspect of the Godhead and he the male aspect. My answer is when you first find love, you then find the power to accomplish the positive.

August 2015 Update

I asked out loud to be shown what to expect shortly after I pass on to the other side. A couple of days later my answer came, an astral projection to my future on the other side.

I found myself sitting in a large and comfortable room, something like you'd expect a lodge located in the mountains to be like. There were many people there none of whom I recognized by their appearance. They were all in their early adulthood. Even though I didn't know them, I felt surrounded by family and lots of love. They were helping me deal with a review of my life while here on Earth.

I heard a loud and very clear voice of a man I had offended. I was very surprised by what he was saying because I had no idea I had hurt him in the way that I had. I then noticed the man who was sitting next to me. I did not recognize his face but I knew that he was a certain family member who had offended me.

From this experience I realize more clearly that relationships with others are so important that we must resolve issues through love and forgiveness before we can move more fully into the Light. And it goes both ways, those we have offended and those who have offended us.

%%% astral projection %%%

While very relaxed and just before sleep, I saw the faces again, one right after the other. They weren't looking at me as before nor did they even seem aware of me. First there were the faces of many men. I couldn't help but wonder where the women were. Once I did this I saw the women, one fading into the next All together there were at least a hundred. Who they are or what this experience means I have no idea. They all seemed to be living a life in the present moment and I was just a brief observer.

This experience has made me much more aware of how connected we are to each other. Our actions and thoughts must, therefore, effect not only ourselves but the whole human race.

%%% astral projection %%%

I was wondering what the "other side" will be like after issues from the physical life are resolved.

As I was deeply meditating on recognizing the Light of God within (as within us all) there appeared a male spirit who took my hand and we flew into many different swirling beautiful colors. The experience lasted a very long time. It was life altering. I never wanted it to end, but the pull of the Earth brought me back to the physical.

%%% astral projection %%%

I have found I can have brief visits to a heaven world (who really knows how many there might be) by first projecting to the tops of trees glistening in the sunlight. I then just look upward. I mostly see beautiful white light in a circular pattern surrounded by gold. This light is so holy it makes my physical body shudder. After a while further outward I can see blue and with some patience the pink both surrounding the gold like rainbows. I do try to bring this awesome light inside of me. It's like receiving a holy communion of light. I believe we are all made of and a part of this wondrous light; we just need to recognize we are.

%%% astral projection %%%

I'm still curious about the afterlife. I now realize that there are many places where we can choose to dwell. I was shown a large crowd of people. I recognized two of my cousins in their younger forms. There was a lot of talking all at once. It was noisy but not uncomfortable. My mother or a spirit posing as my mother left the group. After I saw her, she went back inside. I could see a young child with her. The reason I suspect this spirit was not my real mother is that my mother would have at least smiled at me.

Just like here on Earth, we have free will. We create our own worlds.

%%% astral projection %%%

The easiest way I know to control my dreams is to start by mentally dancing as I doze off. This sometimes brings me to a group of very primitive people where we are dancing around a large fire. We're very pleased with the fire because it will give warmth to us as we sleep and protection from wild beasts. There is clapping of our hands to maintain a rhythm and there is lots of laughter and happiness.

PART FOUR, HOW TO SEE YOUR AURA

Aura, Etheric and Halo Viewing

Seeing your own magnificent light will help you with astral projection because you will realize that a part of you is already outside of your physical body. You will know you are a holy spirit and truly a child of God. It's very exciting, just a matter of waking up the Third Eye which (from my understanding) is located at the center of your forehead and extends to the very center of your head. This teaching originated with the Hindu religion and has been adopted by many others.

When following these instructions you will have one foot in the third dimension (the physical) and one foot in the fourth dimension (the astral). Keep in the back of your mind that on the astral plane space is an illusion and intent is everything.

Beyond practicing the below-listed techniques, three other things you can do to help this skill along include candle-flame gazing, doing the yoga headstand, and paying close attention to colors here in the third dimension.

The best time to practice is just before you go to bed for the evening or when you lay down to take a nap, because later when your eyes are closed and you are relaxed enough to start to doze, you could see some other results of your efforts by spontaneous viewings of spheres of usually brilliant, vibrant rainbow colors or inner-world astral projections.

The instructions I am about to give you will bring a ringing sound which I have explained in previous sections of this book. When this sound gets very intense, some people mistakenly believe they have an inner ear infection. If you want the ringing noise to fade, stop listening for it and it will start to fade, but it is always with us.

Aura viewing can also bring other psychic gifts like the visions of angels and spontaneous very fast flashes of bright colors from higher dimensions including light from your own aura, the aura of a guide, protecting angel, or the light from someone praying for you or wishing you well.

You will not only be able to see your own aura in the mirror but will get spontaneous viewings of other people's auras when you're not even trying. At times, this could be very annoying because you might need instead to stay focused on everyday matters. When this happens, mentally say "no" and then blink your eyes and the view will go away. The more you send these spontaneous viewings away, the less frequently they will occur.

Around your head you will see many different spheres within spheres of different colored light starting with the etheric, your ghost, then the golden halo which we all have, not just the saints. You will also see the aura which has many layers of amazingly beautiful light. There are also thought forms which consist of astral, etheric, and mental matter that we create and build ourselves or that we attract to us because of similar thoughts. It's true what the old saying teaches: "Like attracts like". These thought forms have color, size, shape, and life.

When we view our light, we have one foot in the astral plane where time and space are illusions. So practice done on one day sometimes has an additional effect the next day or even the next week or month with spontaneous viewings.

The light of your aura, being very fluid, changes all the time by blending with other energies. When you are in a group of people it blends with the individual auras of the members of the group. Music can be seen as a thought form moving through your aura. If you have just come from a very scary movie, if family or work problems have come up, if you are sick, these are all things that could create a negative color and energy.

Your most magnificent holy light is located around the top of your head. Located further down the body towards the middle to lower middle you will find less brilliant light reflecting health issues and more mundane things but still very important to you. Towards the bottom say from the knees downward is usually where the garbage is. And most of us have it. Otherwise, we wouldn't need to be here in this classroom called Earth. Down there, some of the things you might find could resemble black and red thunderbolts, snake-like images, and thought forms like the gargoyle statues from the Middle Ages.

Everything in our aura is either our own creation from this life, an alternate self, a past or future life, or energy we have attracted because it is similar to our own. These thought forms have the power to rise and stare into our eyes. And that is what they do when they are influencing us. To see them like I have is quite an awakening experience.

In the above paragraph I deliberately mentioned "future life" because time is an illusion.

I've seen enough of my garbage that I don't even look anymore. I just send light down there and pray for anything negative to be transmuted into the light of God. If you try to look for the negative, you'll find it and get depressed. Our mental institutions and jails are full of people who have seen their own negativity and even talk to it and sometimes it talks back. That's one of the reasons in times past this simple technique had been kept from most people. Think about it. This gift, if misused, could drive you insane.

Our light is recognized subconsciously by close friends and family all the time. They usually know how our presence feels to them. They can sometimes recognize depression and excitement even when we are trying to conceal it. Those close to us have auras that blend with our own very intimately in the fourth and higher dimensions.

You will never forget the first time you start to see your own magnificent light because you will then realize that you are a holy spirit and truly a child of God. It's very exciting. These lights will reveal themselves ever more and more deeply with practice. We all have the ability to see our own light if we apply ourselves.

As I have mentioned in previous sections of this book, the easiest light to see is that of the etheric body. Unless it is reflecting the colors of your aura, your golden halo, your hair, or your clothing, the etheric body is a white light extending about an inch or two on one side and fades in and out. Because of the contrast in color, it shows up more easily around those of us who have dark hair or skin against a white background; and those who are bald or have white or blond hair with light-colored skin, against a dark background. Everyone has this light, our ghost.

In the movies and stories about people who die suddenly but try to stay involved with the Earth plane instead of going on to the light, they are in their etheric bodies. Those dramas are sometimes based on what can actually happen. The spirits who stay behind usually automatically create a body in the image of how they view themselves. It is made from etheric matter which is very abundant. When this etheric light is separated from the physical, and if it is not molded into any particular image, it looks hazy and like the traditional white ghost image of Halloween. These ghost images are sometimes picked up around grave sites. However, when departed people instead go through their tunnel and embrace the light, they are then in their astral or mental bodies and their etheric light just fades away in time.

A problem is that this etheric light and the outline of our heads together can create an after image more pronounced with dark-haired people. It's a good idea while staring at an image when searching for light to glance away periodically so you can separate the illusion from the real. These after images appear when the head moves, when you blink your eyes, and when you look at the aura directly. Proper aura viewing is done with peripheral vision. After images are very beautiful and look like halos of light but eventually they float away.

When your eyes are focused on the astral plane, the atmosphere, the air itself, will look different. You will see small, rapid circular movement. The very air we breathe will appear to be full of life, and indeed it is.

One of the easiest colors to see is gold, because we all have a golden halo, not just the saints. This halo is a sphere of light encompassing and extending from our heads. It doesn't follow the outline of our entire physical body. I'm not saying you don't have an inner sphere of golden light in addition to the halo you might have. If your eyes are focusing on the gold and you see gold everywhere, it's probably because you are looking out through your own halo. So you will not only be seeing lights reflected in the mirror, you will also be looking out through layers of colored lights.

One day, when I was viewing my aura in the mirror, I was amazed that my hair suddenly had a lot of golden highlights that I had never noticed before. Then I realized it was my halo that I was either looking at or through. You'll also see flashes of gold light under your chin, the front side of the bottom of your halo. If your skin suddenly appears more tan than usual, it's probably the halo you're starting to see.

The size of the aura is different for everybody. I have read that the aura of Gautama Buddha extended for several miles. I suspect people who have a strong charismatic personality have larger auras than other people.

Beyond the halo and the etheric light, there is an inner and outer aura. The outer is made of very fine light, very subtle; the inner aura light is more intense. Both contain different spheres of multicolored light and sometimes these spheres contain different colored bands.

Another common color to see that probably everyone has is blue gray, the color mostly associated with the astral plane. When Mother Mary appeared in Medjugorje, it was reported she came in a beautiful mist of blue-gray light.

Around your head and inside the inner aura area, you might find geometric shapes like pyramids and stars of brightly colored more intense light. Because I found they were difficult for me to see at first, I reported that in two of my classes and no one saw any. However in my third class, I forgot to tell them and almost everyone saw them. These are your highest thought forms, composed of astral and mental material.

Just like in the physical, you'll usually find what you're really looking for in your own and other people's auras. For instance, if you are a happy person, you will find beautiful light in yourself and others. If you are depressed or viewing someone who is depressed, you will find charcoal gray. Problems with anger or sex will show as bright red. Health problems will also be reflected as brown, gray, or even black patches. And you might be putting this light there or be helping to magnify it in others yourself. We all affect each other.

There are two things that really bother everybody: pointing fingers and staring. We all instinctively feel the intrusion when receiving this energy from others especially when there is anger. On the other hand, we've all heard stories of people who can heal with their hands. This is because the light from our aura extends from our hands and eyes. The energy that we send out is very real and has a texture and a color.

As I reported earlier, aura viewing is done with peripheral vision. To view the aura, you will be sending out energy because you will be staring very intently. This light that you will be sending out can be seen in a mirror by looking straight ahead. It starts out as a small spiral of colored light; the longer and more intensely we stare, the larger it gets. It is the light in the center of our tunnel. So, of course, after a while our own light going out blends with the aura that is being viewed even in a mirror. If the light you are sending gets too large and distracting, then you need to stop and take a short break.

To be able to identify this light going out and not get it confused with the aura you are viewing, simply turn your eyes to a blank space on the wall. You'll be amazed. Doing this has taught me the importance of my thoughts. One day I was depressed when I was practicing. After staring at my aura for a little while, I looked at a blank space on the wall. I saw charcoal gray.

If your intent is to see your own light in the mirror, be sure to ask any guide or angel to kindly step aside. Otherwise, you could start to see their light as well, if they choose to reveal it to you.

And remember, the wall or ceiling you stare at is just there on the physical plane. On the fourth or even higher dimensions that you will be viewing, the wall might not be there. One day as I was reading a book, I received a spontaneous flash of light. What really amazed me is that the location of the light was behind the book. When I saw the light, I saw through the book.

Start by getting into a very tranquil state. Instead of relaxing by tensing each muscle group separately, save time and do them all at once. Pay special attention to your face muscles. Then roll your neck around slowly first in one direction and then the other. Move your shoulders up and down.

Get very comfortable and secure in your chair. Don't cross your legs or your ankles. Spread your legs a little. Your bottom should feel like the base of a pyramid. Like in astral projection keep your back straight to help control your mind.

You'll be using muscles that probably haven't been used since you were a child. Even though they are small muscles, they can still cause a big strain. If you feel a headache or nausea coming on, take a break.

One of the sacred areas in our astral bodies is called the sun center located in the center of the forehead. When viewing your own aura in the mirror, or when viewing another person's aura, gaze at this sun center and then the aura will present itself through your peripheral vision extending outward from the physical body.

You'll be viewing spheres within spheres of different colored light. You might view one layer; then you blink and you're at a different layer with a different color. It's not an optical illusion. That's how vision on the astral plane works very different from vision on the physical.

Pay attention to any flashes of bright color or geometric shapes when they first start to show themselves and remember where they are located. As you practice, they will appear more and more clearly. The more you study your own aura, the more it will open to you. Glimpses of vague curves seen in the beginning will take shape more clearly with vivid colors and a definite outline with practice.

At first, the golden light from your halo might make colors look muddy around your head. Don't think there's something wrong with you. These colors will clear to your vision in time.

I find that some deep breathing helps me stay energized but yet relaxed. I alternate this deep breathing with periods where I am so relaxed that I hardly breathe at all. I also find that aura viewing is much easier when turned into a spiritual meditation. I have seen the most clearly right after a short prayer. Something like: "Dear God, please reveal Thyself through my aura." Chanting the AUM is also very beneficial.

Twenty years or more ago there was a cartoon character named Mr. Magoo. He lost his glasses a lot and needed to squint and stare to see anything. He had the auric stare down real good. You want to get your eyes slightly out of focus, and then lower your eyelids so that everything but the point of your stare is out of focus. Experiment by moving your head back just a bit but not to the point where you are uncomfortable. When your vision enters the astral plane, you will know you are there because the atmosphere will have motion and life.

If you normally wear glasses or contact lenses, follow your inner guidance. Experiment and see if your auric vision is stronger with or without them.

As you view yourself in a mirror try to keep your head still and don't let your eyes stray from the center of your forehead. These two things in the beginning can seem very difficult especially when you must relax at the same time; by doing so, after images won't be too much of a problem.

You could start by gazing at a candle flame. Mentally deep breathe in the sacred fire of a candle flame. It brings calmness, holiness and a lot like the feeling you have when you're looking at a baby. The candle flame will become your best friend, will help make your world a lot easier, and you will become holier. You might think you don't have the time, but you'll find even fifteen minutes a day makes a big difference in your life

As soon as you start to see the light extending from the candle flame just by looking at it, notice its height, intensity, texture and color. For a couple of minutes don't adjust your eyes in any way, just look at the flame.

Then practice the simple auric stare. First, just stare at the flame, not to the intensity that you see two flames, but adjust your stare to the point just before the flame separates into two. Practice this for a couple of minutes.

You will notice that the light from the flame gets a little bit shorter but more intense. You have penetrated a layer of the flame's aura. Next very slowly lower your eyelids but continue to stare. Slowly move your head backward just a little bit so that the only thing you see is the candle flame and its light.

The rays that extend from your eyeballs to the flame are an optical illusion. The horizontal bands of color are very real being the inner aura of the flame. Slowly straighten out your head and raise your eyelids. Do this several times and notice the difference in the auric light. Also notice, if you can, where your eyelashes might cause a distortion. The air should look to be alive.

Next, open your eyes, stop staring, and observe the light extending from the flame. It will appear different to you than when you first started. It will be more vibrant, the color more clear. It will look different because you have paid intense attention to it. And you have just exercised your Third Eye. This clarity will also happen with human aura gazing. The more you practice, the more you see sometimes without effort.

You will never forget the first time you see your own beautiful, amazing light.

My second book, "Astral Projection Guide, Book Two," is available in the Kindle and paperback versions on Amazon.

I am grateful to you for providing the reason for this book because it has helped me focus on the spiritual side of life, that which is real, the Godhead of great love and happiness. I hope it helps you in this way as well.

Made in the USA
Columbia, SC
17 June 2020